THE AUTOBIOGRAPHY OF
H. LAN THAO LAM

The events described in this book in large part represent the recollections of the author as she experienced them. Some events have been fictionalized for artistic purposes, and certain names have been changed or anonymized for privacy. Dialogue is not intended to represent a word-for-word transcription, but it accurately reflects the author's memory of the meaning and substance of what was said.

Art on cover © Lin + Lam
Used by kind permission of the artists

This book's cover design is an homage to the 1933 cover of Gertrude Stein's *The Autobiography of Alice B. Toklas,* published by Harcourt, Brace and Company, which featured a photograph of Stein and Toklas taken by Man Ray.

ISBN: 978-1-948980-29-6

Library of Congress Cataloging-in-Publication Data
Names: Lin, Lana author
Title: The autobiography of H. Lan Thao Lam / Lana Lin.
Identifiers: LCCN 2024058360 (print) | LCCN 2024058361 (ebook) | ISBN
    9781948980296 paperback | ISBN 9781948980302 ebook
Subjects: LCSH: Lam, H. Lan Thao--Friends and associates | Lin,
    Lana--Friends and associates | Artists--Biography | LCGFT: Biographies
Classification: LCC NX93.L355 L56 2025 (print) | LCC NX93.L355 (ebook) |
    DDC 709.2 [B]--dc23/eng/20250609
LC record available at https://lccn.loc.gov/2024058360
LC ebook record available at https://lccn.loc.gov/2024058361

The publisher wishes to thank Hannah Kofman and Amy Peltz

Design and composition by Danielle Dutton
Printed on permanent, durable, acid-free recycled paper in the United States of America

Dorothy, a publishing project books are distributed to the trade by New York Review Books

Dorothy, a publishing project | St. Louis, MO
DOROTHYPROJECT.COM

THE AUTOBIOGRAPHY OF
H. LAN THAO LAM

•

LANA LIN

DOROTHY, A PUBLISHING PROJECT

TABLE OF CONTENTS

I.
BEFORE I CAME TO NEW YORK

By way of water my life with Lana Lin began.

I was born in Mỹ Tho, Việt Nam. I have in consequence always preferred living in a temperate climate, but it is difficult, even in the U.S., to find a temperate climate and live in it. The intense humidity in Việt Nam compelled me to seek more of it through multiple showers per day. I find myself even now happiest in the vicinity of water. My chin at rest on my parents' windowsill, I spent hours meditating on myriad forms of water descending from the skies—glittering sword-like streaks, fierce torrents, quivering beads clinging to the pane. I recall the wonder of my first snow in Vancouver, how the ice crackled on the window that, like me, was not suited to frigidity.

Lana Lin has told me that her older sister used to stand on the radiator to look out the window, also in Canada. This was when Lana Lin was an infant and presumably too young to enjoy the scenery from the window or stand on the radiator herself. Lana Lin's sister seldom ventured outdoors because she was told it wasn't safe. In the winter she could only spend so long gazing at the outside world, forced to abandon her view when her soles began to burn. A child perched at a windowsill, peering out at the world beyond—how many can identify with this familiar feeling now that digital screens substitute for glass panes, offering a seemingly similar portal into another world?

My mother may have appeared quiet and charming in public, but at home and as a schoolteacher she was strict and stern; she scolded the house plants if they did not grow. Her name is Huỳnh Thị Nga. Canadians have struggled with her name since 1986 when she arrived in North America. My father's father was a Chinese merchant who came from Fukien to Việt Nam by boat. There are no photos of him. I have only seen a pencil drawing, which looks like my fifth uncle. My grandfather was tortured by the French, dragged on the road until his clothes were worn away and the skin on his buttocks exposed. My dad therefore grew up without a father, and his mother and sister were overly protective of him.

I have had no liking for violence and have always enjoyed the pleasures of woodworking and stamp collecting. I am fond of modernist furniture, stone walls, and plants of many varieties—but especially functional ones that most effectively filter the air or repel mosquitoes. I like a view but am not adamant about positioning myself in front of one. I prefer to move about and find my views as I come to them.

It was rain that brought Lana Lin and me together, or rather that marked our togetherness, as it would seem to drizzle or pour every time we saw one another in our early days, and rain often coincides with our dates and anniversaries. The sound of falling water now accompanies daily life in our home on the site of a former sawmill in Connecticut.

The Autobiography of Alice B. Toklas, Gertrude Stein's most popular book, is a gossip column of geniuses, geniuses' wives, and their servants, or those who serve them. It is a chronicle of modernism, and it is a history of sentences, and how Gertrude Stein constructed them, her greatest passion perhaps not Alice so much as the long, precise, well-constructed sentence. In *The Autobiography of Alice B. Toklas*, Gertrude Stein ventriloquizes her own memoir through the ruse of her lifetime companion's tale of their quarter-of-a-century partnership. Should *The Autobiography of H. Lan Thao Lam* be published by 2025, it, too, will commemorate a twenty-five-year history, that of H. Lan Thao Lam and Lana Lin.

The lives of Alice B. Toklas and Gertrude Stein are remote from mine and Lana Lin's in almost every way except that ours also revolve around the arts. Presumably we share our homosexuality as well, theirs as closeted lesbians and ours as openly gender nonconforming queers. Practically none of the smaller details of our lives resemble each other's. Alice B. Toklas entered Gertrude Stein's life through an invitation to Stein's already celebrated Saturday evening dinner, which was cooked by Stein's servant, Hélène. Later Alice B. Toklas and Gertrude Stein would hire at least two Vietnamese cooks, or "a succession" as Alice B. Toklas quips in *The Alice B. Toklas Cook Book*. In *Everybody's Autobiography*, Gertrude Stein states that after trouble with the French, they decided to "have an Indo-Chinaman," and admits to having had so many that she cannot remember them all. Monique Truong would fictionalize these "Indo-Chinese" into the character of Bình in *The Book of Salt*. And this is how I know that my people cooked for Alice B. Toklas and Gertrude Stein; we neither hosted nor were invited to dinner. I once said to Lana Lin that she had no people, so her people, which she does not have, are not even in the kitchen.

Gertrude Stein and Alice B. Toklas's "first Indo-Chinaman," Trac, would lean against the door between the kitchen and dining room and reminisce about when he was a child. Lana Lin has also leaned against the kitchen doorframe—for we have no kitchen door—and chattered about her childhood as I have prepared dinner.

Gertrude Stein gently mocks Trac's diminutive stature, calling him a little man who speaks about when he was a little boy in a village where the circus would come, and she comments in an aside that they do have them, circuses, in Indo-China. Trac also gets a diminutive name. Alice B. Toklas is Alice B. Toklas or Alice Toklas and Gertrude Stein is Gertrude Stein, but Trac is simply Trac. And Nguyen is Nguyen. Or Nguyen might be Nyen, as Gertrude Stein writes in *Everybody's Autobiography*.

Trac "used to see phantoms rise up and rise and rise and rise," although his friend in Indo-China said that there were no longer phantoms in Indo-China since the war.

I, too, have seen phantoms during and after war. I grew up entranced by mythical superheroes whose hair could strangle a demon spirit and ghosts whose tongues could impale the eyes of the living or the dead. The borders between this earthly existence and the netherworld were porous, and so I could identify as easily with mere mortals as with immortals. Those of us who have been ghosted by colonial and imperial rulers may return with a vengeance to retrieve our histories, our own ghost stories. We may rise up and rise and rise and rise.

Alice B. Toklas reports that Trac's sole deficiency when he enters their service is that he makes few and simple desserts. He later inexplicably learns how to bake. Perhaps one of the reasons why Trac is initially weak on desserts is because Vietnamese tend to eat fruit for dessert. Our desserts are given to us wholly prepared by nature. We are subject to their seasonal growth. Their vulnerability to the climate makes them precious, for they cannot be enjoyed when one has ventured too far afield of the territories where they can flourish. The most fragile fruits cannot survive transport to the cold regions of the north and west. This was one of the biggest sacrifices in my young life when I irrevocably departed Việt Nam for Canada. How to explain the taste of mangosteen to someone who has never broken into it and dyed their fingertips magenta? How to describe the texture of *vú sữa*—or star apple—to those who have never scooped out its pulp and cradled it on their tongues? Can one conjure the aroma of sapodilla for people who have not been seduced by its fragrance?

While I could not relate to director Trần Anh Hùng's romanticized exoticism of French colonial and postcolonial Việt Nam, yet like the character in *The Scent of Green Papaya*, I too savored fruits in my childhood that have lingered in my senses throughout my life. Consuming fruit satisfies cravings beyond nourishment. Fruit has taught me lessons beyond the manual dexterity it takes to handle the knife needed to access its rewards. I learned patience in waiting for its proper ripening, attention to detail in judging the tautness of its skin or its mellow or acrid smell, and sensitivity to the sound it would emit upon tapping or thumping—a hollow resonance or flat thud. It may seem strange, but my future calling as an artist might have originated with my ardor for fruit.

In Việt Nam, sapodilla is called *sa pô chê*, possibly a transliteration of *chico zapote*, as it is known in its native southern Mexico, or *Manilkara zapota*, its botanical name. The first time I encountered this delectable fruit, I was gravely warned not to swallow the hard, black seeds embedded in it because their sharp hooks could pierce my throat. This may be why my child ears heard *sa pô chê* as *sao cô chê*, which translates as "why" (*sao*) and "dislike" or "disapprove" (*chê*). In substituting *cô* for *pô*, I understood the innocent fruit asking why others disliked or disapproved of her. In the four decades since I have been able to relish the taste of *sa pô chê—sao cô chê* to me—I have carried its meanings with me: that enjoyment comes at the cost of proper care and restraint, but also that the innocent may suffer harm or rejection.

Every evening Lana Lin and I share a palette cleanser of fruit that is equally a ritual of cleansing ourselves of the day in preparation for the next. We have shared pomelo, which I cut apart and place on my head like a wig that makes me look like the cartoon character Dora; watermelon, which remained Lana Lin's favorite as a child despite her ballet instructor telling her that her protruding belly looked as if she had swallowed the entire gourd whole; Macouns and Winesaps, not the red and golden "delicious" apples with a waxed-car sheen stacked in uniform rows in the chilled aisles of supermarket chains that Lana Lin grew accustomed to as a kid; and persimmon, whose squat, glossy, ruddy cheeks add color and flavor to the winter months.

Our first summer together was marked by a mango, the first of many summers and mangos we'd share. Lana Lin regarded mangos as a luxury, but they were so abundant in my childhood as to be commonplace. Expertly peeling a mango or any tropical fruit is second nature to me. I never regarded this as a skill until the first and last time I saw, to my horror, Lana Lin take a potato peeler to a mango. One could not rightly call it peeling. It was closer to abuse. In her untrained hands, the poor mango cried out to me to save it from further disfigurement. We made an instant contract that she would never again commit such a violation of a fruit's tender flesh. She therefore never consumes a mango without me, unless she buys them from the Dominican street sellers in Washington Heights, precut and sprinkled with lime. Alone, she is allowed berries of all kinds; papaya, which can be scooped out after only one painless slice; and watermelon, on which she wielded a rusty meat cleaver until I confiscated it.

Through the voice of Alice B. Toklas, Gertrude Stein remarks that their meeting initiated a "new full life." There is some truth to this as well in terms of my life with Lana Lin. Although I do not consider my life prior to meeting Lana Lin as less full or impoverished, certainly there was a newness in living life as two rather than as one. I confess that I find appealing Plato's myth about lovers as two halves originating from a once androgynous whole. Perhaps I should say that a different shape to life formed with Lana Lin, a shape that my Buddhist belief in past lives recognizes as having been formed before.

II.

MY ARRIVAL IN NEW YORK

On February 25, 2000, after three days of deliberation, a jury in Albany acquitted all four officers who had fired forty-one shots at an unarmed Amadou Diallo, striking him nineteen times, when he pulled out a wallet that they mistook for a gun. The streets of New York City erupted in protest. I was visiting the city to attend the College Art Association conference, what was known colloquially as the meat market for academic teaching jobs in the arts. As I left the Hilton, I could hear chanting, whistling, and banging, and then I was commingling with people raising their fists, wallets clenched in them. Walking along Broadway I caught sight of Violet. We embraced in the middle of the street, each thankful to have found a friend amid the throng of strangers. Together we fell into the rhythm of the marchers, and I noticed among our group a small, somewhat androgynous, somewhat femme Asian person whom I had already seen a couple of times on my brief trip to the Big Apple.

I was fascinated by Lana Lin's hair, which appeared to have a natural curl to it, an unusual feature for East Asian hair. I am particularly observant about hair quality, texture, and cut because I trained in Vidal Sassoon and Japanese techniques and worked as stylist in my post–high school days. The previous night I had attended an event at which Lana Lin sat directly in front of me. For some reason, she had decided to pile all her hair on the top of her head, something she has never done since in the twenty-plus years we have lived together. Later I learned she had never performed such a feat upon her hair at any prior time in her life. She had been possessed that night by the urge to pull her hair up, for seemingly no reason at all, except that I might then sit behind her staring at the slight curls that lined the nape of her neck, which was slim and graceful to my eyes. I would not have suspected then that I would be taking my shears to that nape every four to eight weeks over the next two decades or more, save for a year in which chemotherapy took over. There is an incredible intimacy in giving a person a haircut. It is an experience almost every human goes through at the hands of another, not unlike sex, although for some sex involves greater mutuality. Certainly within the haircutting dyad, the giver and receiver are distinctly defined, seldom if ever changing positions.

I cannot recall if we missed Al Sharpton's speech by the time we reached City Hall. It was getting dark and we were hungry. We headed to a Thai place just below Canal that was the go-to spot for that group, which was made up almost entirely of Whitney Museum Independent Study folks, meaning critically engaged artists, curators, and critics of a Stuart Hall/Raymond Williams/David Harvey sort. Lana Lin and I were probably the only interlopers, although we, too, subsequently joined the cult. In the weeks to follow, Lana Lin confessed that one of the reasons she fell in love with me was the rapture with which I ordered deep-fried tofu, that and the abandon with which I had embraced Violet on the street, an embrace she envied and envisioned between the two of us even then.

We might have been waiting for a table, or lingering before the next phase of the evening, but we were all standing around on the street, as we often did at that time, in a loose collective after events, screenings, performances, and talks, before next steps were decided—shall there be drinks, who is walking which direction, is anyone else taking the A train, does anyone want to share a cab? In the semidarkness I could not see Lana Lin and pondered aloud, "Where's Lana?" She had wandered off to check her messages and heard that her new nephew had been born the previous night. I wonder, if one were to examine the confluences of any given day, whether one would always find a set of seemingly significant coincidences: a birth, a death, the start of a lifelong love affair, another benchmark in a history of racial injustices.

After this propitious meeting, I returned to my parents' house in Mississauga, Ontario, where I was living at the time, and my lengthy bike rides to and from Toronto, where I worked at an outdoor athletic gear store. Before too long, Lana Lin contrived to come to Toronto for a film festival that was showing a short film she had made five years prior. She called me from a payphone at Union Station and asked what I was doing over the Easter weekend. I said I was moving stones in my mother's garden, and we made a plan to have dinner at Lee Garden before her screening. When she appeared in the restaurant, she was wearing the smallest leather biker jacket I had ever seen. It was well worn and looked several years older than she. I was so nervous that I ordered a dish called a bird's nest, something I would typically never do and have never done since. It was painfully dry, making it difficult, in my anxiety, to swallow. I fixated on Lana Lin's scarlet lipstick, which she later told me she had hurriedly applied on the street while rushing to meet me. It was Chanel. It was the one designer label she invested in, even though she tended to wear lipstick only on special occasions. During the cancer year she switched to organic, and now she wears lipstick even less frequently.

I felt myself panicking during the screening as I tried to formulate a response to what I was viewing. The film was beyond me, but I recognized it as related to those of Trinh T. Minh-ha, a filmmaker and writer I respected. However, the rapid-fire pace of Lana Lin's *Stranger Baby* made it even more obtuse than other experimental films I had seen. After the screening, or maybe it was during, Lana Lin whispered, "I need a drink." I was happy to comply. We went for a whisky and then sauntered in the rain searching for cheesecake, which we eventually found at Future

Bakery on Bloor Street. Intermittently, droplets clinging to the balustrades of overhead balconies unleashed themselves on my forehead as I reminisced about playing soccer on our open terrace in Sài Gòn during monsoon season.

We were five girls screaming and laughing, barefoot on the slick red-and-white ceramic tiles. More than once we narrowly missed slipping and causing ourselves mortal injury. This was the terrace that I studied with my chin pressed on the ledge of my parents' large picture window, head cocked to the right, a habit I had never been conscious of until I noticed it in several photographs. The rain in Sài Gòn was both mesmerizing and cruel, often forming a barrier between me and the outside world. On that day, not long after the war ended, we had been locked inside for weeks. Our parents feared our disappearance, a fate suffered by others on our block, but Mom was so weary of the restless presence of her pent-up children that she didn't bother to call us back when one of us dashed into the storm to retrieve the ball that had, on its own, ventured through the propped-open door, as if it, too, was itching to be set free. The thump of a punt, muffled as it was by the lashing of the downpour, was a bell struck, and the rest of us streamed outside as if class was over. We hollered and ran with abandon, strands of sopping hair blinding us. From time to time, I gulped the warm water pooling in my gaping mouth. When Mom finally needed someone to roast sweet potatoes while she went for the second, third, or fourth time to secretly exchange the rest of her cash for gold before it completely lost its value, we begrudgingly padded inside like a herd of wet dogs.

The last of the pack, I swiped a precious *vú sữa* from the low-hanging branch that arched over our terrace walls. *Vú sữa* translates literally to "breast milk," so named because of the way the juice breaches the cut surface of the fruit. Perhaps because my mom had had so little of it for me, I craved the creamy delicacy. I had been told not to fuel the neighbors' animosity, but the rare seasonal fruit dangled tantalizingly within reach. I couldn't resist the purple-tinted green globe. Technically, I justified to myself, it's on my family's property, or above it, and inaccessible to our neighbors.

I often watched the family next door from my parent's second-floor window, where I could see everything going on in their backyard. The grandfather was a woodworker, and I was transfixed by the intricate curls that bubbled up from his plane, floating gently into a pile at his sandaled feet. If there was a breeze, the swirls would dance on the concrete with the leaves. When the war ended, these neighbors immediately raised a Việt Cộng flag. We had never suspected that they were spies for the North, since the woman was District Head. As a member of the victors' party, she continued to serve as District Head after the Fall of Saigon. The shock of these everyday duplicities taught us to distrust even, perhaps especially, people close to you—though somehow I always trusted Lana Lin, and I was not wrong to do so.

That first drizzly evening in Toronto I may have revealed to Lana Lin my fondness for salt-and-pepper hair, which I had once glimpsed from our balcony terrace in Sài Gòn where I would stand, leaning over the wall and peering at the worldly activity below. An elegant elderly man in a crisp white shirt rode his bicycle past our house. That glimpse struck me as the sexiest moment I had yet experienced in my young life. And I knew, in that instant: *That's the person I want to be.*

Lana Lin spent the next rainy day rambling on Queen Street. In the evening she attended a screening and after-party where she stood uncomfortably in a lobby packed with people she did not know. As she exited the theater and was headed to a bus stop, a man ran up and jumped on her from behind. He started to hump her, and she struggled to keep walking. In the distance Lana could see an Asian woman she had just met at the festival. The man ran off and maybe Lana waved to her. Or maybe Lana waved and the man ran off. Or maybe the woman waved and the man ran off. The woman began to approach with a quizzical look on her face. But Lana pretended as if nothing had happened, and the woman turned away. When Lana recalls this incident, it reminds her of other incidents that have become entangled with it in a web of associations.

Once when she was wedged into a subway car during rush hour a man jerked himself off against her. She tried to move away from him, but the car was too crowded. She turned her eyes away in disgust and rested them upon an older white woman seated in the spot reserved for disabled and elderly riders. The woman asked if Lana wanted to take her seat. Lana pushed toward her but did not take the seat. It was enough to get away from the man.

Another event that comes to Lana's mind is related to her reflex to pretend nothing out of the ordinary has happened or is happening. Lana attributes this to the injunction, passed on by her parents both verbally and otherwise, to appear "normal" at all costs, not to stand out in any way other than through academic accolades, to assume the posture of the "model minority," which was to do well but not too well, essentially to disappear into the dominant culture.

The parks and recreation services in Naperville, Illinois, where Lana grew up, would host summer activities, including a "Gold Rush" in which Lana participated when she was around ten years old. A young white gym coach sort of man droned on about how to play the game. The main objective was, predictably, to collect as much gold as possible. More nuanced were the rules of sportsmanship. You couldn't pull a brick out of another kid's hand, for instance, or take one out of their bucket. But there was a hazy area. What if you spotted a brick and were headed toward it, was it fair for someone else to descend upon it before you laid hands on your find? Lana was still unclear about this when the whistle blew. She scampered around like everyone else, spied a brick and took hold of it. As her palm grew sweaty with the weight of the gold, her neck prickled from the pressure of a hostile stare. Had the boy glaring at her already made a claim upon the treasure? Lana let the brick slip out of her grip and heard it hollowly hit the pavement. And then she trudged away without looking back, as if this child's play was of no concern to her.

Over the decades, as this inconsequential event has retreated further from retrievable memory, Lana has not infrequently felt that she was undeserving of a yearned-for object that was within, or literally in, her grasp. It is as if an invisible force strangled her, both in this childhood game and throughout her life. The apprehension that an object she had sought or attained was not rightfully hers was restrictive. She adhered to self-imposed rules that required her to act nonchalant, impervious, covering over any interior distress. Above all, she was not to make her wish or disappointment or rage or shame visible to the outside world.

When Lana tells me about her wave to the onlooking Asian woman—or maybe it was the other way around, even Lana can't be sure—my mind goes to how I waved to her for some unknown reason when we were standing in a group on the street during that fateful NYC visit. I felt a tug to signal to the only other Asian in our gathering, as an invitation, a gesture toward solidarity. Lana waved in return, although she doesn't like to admit that she can't recall this action. Just as her doubt persists as to whether she hailed the other Asian woman in Toronto or responded to her wave, she cannot recollect mirroring me. Perhaps the prohibition against being singled out, or singling herself out, even to accept what is given, causes her to suppress her memories. That may be why I am writing this autobiography.

As the autobiographer-detective, I have rifled through Lana's old writing and uncovered a short story titled "Gold," dated 1/10 /93:

A piece of gold fell from her fingers. She is one who would let the precious slip through her fingers because she is afraid. This moment took place when she was eight years old, but nearly twenty years later, the same laws of gravity apply. Fiercely self-protective, when threatened, rather than cling, she is inclined to fling, to relinquish all desires. It is an animal instinct, like creatures who burrow into sand or play dead when danger signals. Unequipped for confrontation, without fangs or horns, lacking scales or venom, she has not inherited the capacity of the predator.

In the spirit of the scientist she never became, she routinely inspects herself beneath a mental microscope. From an overhead perspective, she observes a deeply tanned, stringy figure, furtive like a mouse or gerbil. Claw hands spring open. An object, glittering in the harsh sun, falls to the concrete playground. The object is obscured by the child's flared skirt, a skirt so white it is painful to examine under the glaring light; it inflicts a headache like the kind she suffered when she gulped a glass of milk too fast.

The gold is lost. The girl hesitantly edges away, tossing her head so her jet-black bangs swing from her sweaty brow. Her hair, like the tar on the driveway, feels scorched by Midwestern summers. Before her plastic soles take two steps from the shimmering brick, an alabaster, closely shaved head bounds toward it. Blue-striped T hurtles, dirt-smudged fingers snatch. "I found it! It's mine! I've got SEVEN pieces of gold. I'm going to win the treasure hunt. I'm going to win!" The voice howls as rubber pounds away on the pavement.

Her mind shuffles through a series of overexposed images that reveal yet another version of the same event. She discerns bone-thin, bird-like hands pinned against a brick wall, held firmly at the wrist. One talon clutches a golden wedge; the other grasps at air, tearing at eyes it cannot reach. A jarring pinkish-white head rears into the picture.

"Give me that gold, you nigger."

"I'm not a nigger," she peeps.

"Chink, what difference does it make? Give it to me, coolie."

"No, I'm not. I found it. It's mine."

"Give it to me or I'll peek under your skirt. I bet you're not wearing any panties."

"I am, too," she whines.

"I bet you're not."

"I am," she cries.

"Let me see." He releases her ringed wrists and tears at her skirt, smearing it with baloney and mustard sandwich remains. Although she is wearing uncomfortably bulky shorts because boys were forever trying to flip up girls' skirts at recess, she thrusts it down with both hands, letting her block of gold fall. He pounces —a slab of meat to a prowling lion—and races off, roaring. "The coolie has no panties on! The coolie has no panties on!"

She turns her inner lens, blinking her eyes to focus. Her forehead is creased. She is vexed that she cannot extinguish this scalding treasure hunt. It swarms, vibrating about her, an unrelenting mosquito. She slams her palms together, ready to peel it away, bloody and limp. She will blow gently so it will drop nimbly to her feet. She could sweep it aside with her slippered toe and be rid of it forever. But she hasn't discovered its weakness, the key to its extermination. It is a monster with many lives, and she despairs that she can never overcome it. Baring her teeth, she snarls, "This is my reward, to which I am entitled, that I won of my own accord. Through cunning I have deciphered its worth; through strength shall I keep and shelter it. Indestructible, this precious element shall fortify me all the rest of my life." She squints, urging the vision to clarify. Still, she cannot scrutinize this revision of history. Neither scientist nor alchemist, she is too timid to dally with invention. She survives as an animal driven by primordial hunger, through instinct, to hunt for gold.

Enough of the details of this short story comport with memories Lana has relayed to me that I perceive in this fiction an amalgam of her lived experiences. In my mind, the microscope Lana conjures functions more like a telescope through which I survey her past. I detect the eight- or ten-year-old introvert upon whom I superimpose the thirty-four-year-old with whom I fell in love and the fifty-seven-year-old with whom I am growing into the salt-and-pepper gentleman I once dreamed of becoming. I cannot fathom her a wild animal. She is more like my beloved fruit, its tender vulnerability encasing an enduring kernel. Yet, while humankind distresses her, she can call up the courage to confront certain situations that are difficult for me. Phoning a utility company is daunting, ordering in noisy restaurants harrowing, asking for directions in a foreign country terrifying, yet Lana can envisage possibility in the face of apparent impossibility. She can shape an inchoate sprawl of ideas and feelings into coherence; she will not give up on catching a train until it is literally pulling out of the station without her; she refuses to forsake seemingly doomed projects, such as finding an affordable dwelling within two hours of New York City at the height of a pandemic. Though not entitled, she is resolute in her conviction that we deserve our share in the world, despite evidence to the contrary. Like the milk fruit I cherish that harbors potentially deadly seeds, if one treats her with respect and care, Lana Lin can secrete a vitalizing potion.

On Easter Sunday, Lana waited over an hour for me to arrive at Future Bakery on Queen Street. She had plenty of time to read on the menu that the business started when the owner's Ukrainian grandmother and Polish grandfather fled the Red Army. Lana's and my immigrant histories echo this family's: they sought a better future in the West. It occurs to me now that in meeting up at these two Futures, our own two futures became indelibly entwined.

It was Lana's last day in Toronto before she headed back to NYC. Cell phones were not yet common, and neither of us had them. Running late and stuck in traffic, I did not know if she would still be at the cafe when I showed up. She was, and we commenced a conversation that would go on unbroken for eight hours. We went for a stroll along Lake Ontario, walking and talking about what we wanted and did not want in life. I dreamed of living in a barn one day. I always thought I would be alone. Neither of us wanted children. The brisk sunny day turned to dusk, and Lana relieved herself in the trees off the path while I watched for oncoming pedestrians. This is when I knew we were suited to each other. Lana concluded that she wanted to share her life with me when we went for congee later that night and I carefully cleaned first her utensils and then mine with hot tea before our steaming bowls arrived. The next

day Lana went back to her tenure-track job teaching film editing and digital postproduction at the City College of New York.
I would soon be off backpacking with several Canadian men
who boasted substantial strides. I had scheduled a seven-day
trek, taking advantage of my Mountain Equipment Co-op em-
ployee discount. I'd like to say that I basked in my newfound
love in those first weeks, but I was too busy trying to keep pace
with the lanky outbackers. When I finished the trek, at least
a dozen dehydrated food packs later, I devoured a gigantic,
greasy fish and chips dinner and dialed Lana to report that I
had survived.

On October 24, 1934, when Gertrude Stein reached the New
York harbor for her U.S. tour, flush with the success of *The Autobiography of Alice B. Toklas*, an electric sign in Times Square
flashed: "Gertrude Stein Has Arrived." No such signage marked
my arrival in New York City. Rather, a series of moments, assessed in retrospect, accumulate into the beginnings of my
piecemeal, unplanned migration to the U.S.:

Spilling an entire container of miso soup on Lana's futon
the first night I stayed over, the balled-up sheets glowing under
the blue TV screen she had set up through her VCR for mood
lighting.

Spontaneously pulling into a drive-in movie theater at the
end of a camping trip, firing up our propane tank, boiling ra-
men noodles and a zucchini with the last of our gas.

Playing a video of me modeling a bright blue coat I found for Lana at Winners in Mississauga. She laughed so hard and still wears the coat twenty-four years later.

The microwave committing suicide, taking two stove dials with it as it fell off a shelf while we argued over something we have both forgotten.

Peering over my tower of popcorn, searching for Lana in the darkened crowd of the Ziegfeld, the smell of salted butter wafting into my nostrils.

Canoeing on Paradox Lake with a little too much vigor, falling asleep with mummified arms, waking up the next morning unable to give Lana a celebratory birthday hug.

Discovering that the nurse who sublet our apartment one summer consumed a bag of fortune cookies with bespoke messages that we'd designed for an art project. Lana, indignant, complaining, "If someone eats your art, they should pay for it, or at least apologize."

Attending a free screening of *Manhattan* at the United Palace, the postmodern tour de force of orientalism in Washington Heights, outfitted in our most dazzling dapper attire for "wear a suit" day.

Raising the appliance like a trophy while I announce: "I love New York, the only place where you can find a professional hair dryer at a corner store on a Saturday at midnight!"

Helping Lana haul a five-drawer steel filing cabinet from Chinatown up five flights while she anxiously muttered that she had never owned anything she couldn't carry on her own, though she had to admit we needed the storage space. My labor gained me access to a drawer that held my meager belongings within the 450-square foot apartment in which Lana had stashed her accumulation of a dozen years of New York City living.

III.
LANA LIN IN NEW YORK, 1988–1999

Lana Lin came to New York City in 1988 and lived there off and on, mostly on, for the next thirty-two years. After graduating from the University of Iowa with a BA in Communications, she had no plan for adulthood and took a road trip west with her two sisters. She spent a miserable summer in California that spurred her to move to New York with Matthew, whom she had met and started seeing in Iowa. Even back then, Lana was averse to calling anyone her "boyfriend." Her discomfort was not with the term's explicit gender or implicit sexual orientation—I was never her "girlfriend," nor was she mine—but the word seemed juvenile to her, even though she was, in fact, young. Despite Lana's rejection of the term, Matthew could safely have been called Lana's "boyfriend" when she came to New York for the first time since she and her sisters had visited during her high school's winter break.

Matthew found their first residence from an ad in the *Village Voice* before Lana even arrived. It was a studio apartment on Eleventh Street between Avenues A and B, right next door to what was once a public bathhouse, which Lana hardly remembers although she must have stridden past it almost every day for a year. Designed by Arnold W. Brunner and built between 1904 and 1905, the building stands a couple of stories shorter than the surrounding buildings but nevertheless exudes stature due to its neo–Italian Renaissance style, its lofty arched windows over three entrances, and the bold inscription—FREE PUBLIC BATHS OF THE CITY OF NEW YORK—carved into its light-colored Indiana limestone and flanked on either side by two decorative carvings ornamented with fish whose bodies form a loose heart shape with heads facing one another and tails intertwining around a trident. As I have often remarked to Lana, the facade of a building is its public face and its windows are its eyes. One walks through its mouth to enter its interior.

But the bathhouse on Eleventh Street had more than one mouth. A 1934 photograph of the building from the New York Public Library reveals a girl entering the right side of the frame heading toward the entrance on the right, while on the far left of the frame four boys stand behind a man in a suit and boater hat, staring at the other entrance. Men and women were segregated upon entry, hence the three arched entrances, the center for a central office. In 1911, 427,557 patrons used the sixty-seven showers and two bathtubs designated for men and the twenty-seven showers and five bathtubs designated for women. Public bathhouses were meant to serve the poor, who tended to be immigrants.

538 East Eleventh Street closed as a bathhouse in 1958 and was used as a garage and warehouse until the mid 1990s. Matthew habitually voiced his suspicion that behind the steel rolling gates covered with graffiti something other than the storing

and transporting of beer and soda pop must be going on. Of every desolate spot in the city that somehow subsisted without any rational, visible means, Matthew would say, "It must be a drug ring." It wasn't until Lana and I binge watched *Breaking Bad* that she understood what Matthew meant, or at least she could see how a beverage warehouse could be a cover for a meth lab on TV.

In 1995 the building was bought by the Pulitzer Prize–winning photographer Eddie Adams for $475,000 and cleaned up for fashion and corporate photography. The property, now known as Bathhouse Studios, hosted events for such clients as Gucci, Nike, Ford, and Lamborghini. In 2018, it sold for $16.25 million.

I was born in the south of Việt Nam, a little over a month after Eddie Adams took one of the defining photographs of the Vietnam War. *Saigon Execution*, the photograph for which Adams won the Pulitzer Prize, captures Brigadier General Nguyễn Ngọc Loan firing a bullet into the skull of Captain Nguyễn Văn Lém. In his essay "Five Famous Asian War Photographs," Amit Majmudar comments on this visual depiction of "*literally*, an unarmed man getting shot," though Majmudar misidentifies the victim as a civilian, perhaps because, in addition to being unarmed, he lacks a military uniform. The shooting (in both senses) took place on Ngô Gia Tự Street, Chợ Lớn quarter (Chinatown), Sài Gòn, now Hồ Chí Minh City. You have most likely seen this unforgettable image, but the photograph is such a visual assault that its subtleties may have bypassed you. The brutality shocks one into glossing over details, thinking one has captured the photo in a single knowing glance. For instance, one might not notice the shadow on the street at the lower right corner of the frame, and that it is sharper than the shadows of trees that fill the space beneath Loan's outstretched hand holding his snub-nosed revolver. When I forced myself to study the photo, I initially thought that this shadow sneaking to the right of the prisoner might have been cast by the photographer. But this would have been impossible given the angle of the light. Then I thought it might have been cast by the NBC News cameraman who was also on site; the protruding oblong shape atop a more rounded shape somewhat emulates a camera with onboard mike. In researching this photo, however, I stumbled across a contact sheet upon which the full-frame negatives were printed. It revealed that the shadow was of a man who is frequently cropped out, wearing a light-colored cap and pants. His face cannot be seen. He appears almost to stroll along the path of the gunfire, though the prisoner was between him and the general, blocking him from harm.

There is film footage of the execution, shot by Võ Sửu, the NBC cameraman, and yet it is the frozen image of the moment of death that is fixed and fixated upon in the public archives of trauma. A photograph tears an image out of its context within the life-stream of images, preserves it in perpetuity, or an approximation thereof. I won't rehearse the well-known theories about the work that photographic images do, what Susan Sontag, Roland Barthes, and so many others—Ariella Azoulay, Tina Campt, Sharon Sliwinski—have already said. I will only comment on the contrast in this case between the film footage and the photograph. The moving image almost trivializes the execution, which occurs so quickly and unceremoniously that the man walking past the event, who is so often cropped out of the photograph, doesn't have a chance to turn around until after Captain Nguyễn has collapsed onto the pavement. The still image doesn't so much trivialize Nguyễn's death as confer gravitas on the violence, severing it from the chaos of actuality. But both documents have in common what Sontag famously observes: "There is aggression implicit in every use of the camera." Adams himself has said: "Photography by its nature is selective. It isolates a single moment, divorcing that moment from the moments before and after that possibly lead to adjusted meaning." But everything is selective, even nature. Memory is selective. As I write this autobiography, I isolate moments that I can remember, divorcing them from other moments, and my life changes, its meanings change as I remember and misremember.

I was born on March 9, 1968 during the Tet Offensive, the coordinated North Vietnamese attacks timed to coincide with the Lunar New Year on January 30, 1968. With the nightly bombings and fear that the Việt Cộng would enter homes and take prisoners in the weeks before my birth, it became a ritual that my dad would sleep at a hotel or someone else's house, and each night my mom would go to the hospital. It was 4 A.M. when I slipped out of my mom's womb. The smooth delivery was likely paved by the five siblings who preceded me, four of whom survived. My mom says little about my birth aside from reporting her thirst. My dad was told about my arrival, but when he got to the hospital he was inconsolable at still being bereft of a son. He took out a notebook and scribbled the list my mom dictated: diapers, milk, food, and water. Then he went home and fell asleep. Meanwhile my mom and I both went hungry; she had very little milk for me. My dad's disappointment was compounded by the fortune tellers who had wrongly predicted my sex, yet part of me has always wondered if they were right. I went through life feeling that I ought to have been a boy.

During those early years in New York City, Matthew and Lana ambled from one side of Manhattan to the other. Having grown up in a suburban cocoon, Lana was astonished to discover that in real life the brownstones and even the garbage cans really did look like *Sesame Street*, and shop owners and cabbies really did sound like characters in Woody Allen movies.

After Eleventh Street, Lana and Matthew lived on Fifth Street between First and Second Avenues, down the block from the 9th Precinct of the NYC Police Department. Late one evening, when the two of them were in their apartment, Matthew heard a sharp snap. He dashed down the stairs to see the empty pole where he normally locked his bike. He trudged back upstairs, depressed, and rose the next morning earlier than usual, resentful that he wouldn't have his bike for his morning commute. As he approached Second Avenue, he saw his bike ride by.

"Hey, do you want to sell that bike?" he yelled.

The rider hesitated. "Sure, I'll sell it for two hundred dollars."

Though this was more than he had paid for it, Matthew consented, but said he needed to go home to get some cash. As the two turned onto Fifth Street, the man grew nervous and stopped.

"I'm not going any farther," he grumbled.

"Well, I just want it because it's my bike," Matthew genially replied. Taken aback, the man agreed to return the bike to its original owner for the twenty dollars Matthew had in his pocket.

When Lana met Matthew in Iowa City, she was certain he was gay. He wore suit jackets and bow ties, round black glasses, and would attend film screenings at the Bijou with his best friend, Chip, also in suit jacket and bow tie. Everyone thought the flamboyant pair, whose effervescent laughter could be heard erupting from the back rows of the theater, was a couple. When I met

Matthew, I thought he was just another of the skinny, geeky, tall white boys who would sidle up to Lana at film screenings. Lana rejects my contention that they had crushes on her, but she does admit that white boys or white men are more likely to approach her in a group setting than Asian dykes. As it turns out, Matthew is straight, and Lana is not, but I have embraced Matthew as part of our queer family.

For the first few years after Lana and Matthew split as a couple, they continued to see each other seemingly as much as they had when they were living together. After the breakup, Lana left Manhattan for a while—living in Brooklyn Heights and Williamsburg—before moving back to the East Village in 1993, to an apartment on Thirteenth Street, where she lived alone in New York City for the first time. Living alone in an imposing metropolis felt momentous to Lana. She worried in particular about how she'd change the ceiling light bulbs, which she could not reach even with the new stepladder she'd bought. When Matthew couldn't stop by to perform this task, she would balance the ladder atop a small table he'd made for her, miraculously avoiding a tumble onto the uneven floorboards. Additionally, there was a daunting steel gate covering the window onto the fire escape. Though she appreciated that it was a necessary security measure, Lana had to throw all her weight into the metal contraption in order to swing it open. She wondered if she would have the strength to do this in an actual emergency, with smoke filling her lungs, for example, or with an intruder in the apartment.

In 1980 the artist collective Group Material opened an exhibition entitled *Alienation* in the storefront space of the same building on Thirteenth Street that Lana moved into in 1993. By the time Lana lived there, however, the storefront space had been converted to a laundromat. Lana used to lug her laundry up and down the stairs of her fifth-floor walk-up. Practically every time she did laundry, which was approximately every two weeks, she saw the Asian woman who lived down the hall, who never seemed to stop doing laundry for her family who occupied an apartment on the floor below as well. Lana figured out that they rented two apartments, because the father would shuffle downstairs with only his slippers on. Over the decade that she lived there, Lana almost never spoke to any of her neighbors beyond a monosyllabic greeting. Yet at the laundromat she would greet the woman, who Lana believed to be Chinese but whose name she had never learned, and ask how she was doing. The woman would offer a rejoinder in a cheerfully exasperated tone, something about being busy, tired, or having lots of work or laundry to do. Lana would smile and nod and commiserate with a sympathetic "yeah." If it went the other way around and the woman spoke first, Lana would answer with similar phrases as the woman had on other occasions, and the woman would smile and nod, or more often laugh because despite having so much work and so little time she was very good humored.

Lana is fairly certain that she secured her lease for her apartment because she is Taiwanese. The broker was Asian, and there were several Asians living in the building. The family down the hall had three sons. One would grow up to be an EMT, which Lana ascertained when he started to wear a uniform. Lana only ever knew anything about the people in the building from passing them as she went up and down the five flights of stairs. There was a Latina girl who went from prepubescent to pregnant. There was a very old Asian woman who rented #16, right below Lana's, who rarely left her apartment. Once, when the door was left slightly ajar, Lana peeked in and saw the stove and cabinets covered in greasy, charred foil and the paint peeling from the tin ceiling above.

Late one night, the man down the hall knocked on Lana's door on behalf of the elderly woman from #16 to report a leak apparently coming from Lana's apartment. He implored Lana to take a look downstairs, which made no sense to her. "What good would it do?" she sighed. "You should call the super."

"It will give you a better idea should anyone ask," he asserted.

Out of nowhere the woman from down the hall leaned into Lana's apartment and admired her Brita pitcher, inquiring as to where she bought the filters. Then the super turned up and busied himself in her bathroom. As they all finally filed out, the super touched Lana's shoulder with dirty hands. She recoiled, fearing blackened flannel smudging her freshly laundered sheets.

Like me, Lana had not intended on making her home in New York, nor had she imagined identifying as a New Yorker. She had not dreamed all her life of being at the center of the art world, as Matthew had. She had not been inculcated into a mythology of the great city, nor had she counted on the promises it held and withheld. When she moved to New York, she had not yet read Joan Didion's 1967 essay "Goodbye to All That," nor would she read Eula Biss's homonymous 2005 reimagining of it until having lived in the city for over three decades. Like Didion and Biss, Lana began her tenure in New York at a young age; they twenty and twenty-one, she twenty-two. But unlike Didion and Biss, Lana stayed. Listening to Biss's essay and then reading Didion's, and then reading Biss's essay and listening to it again, Lana asks herself why she stayed and they left.

Lana did not move to NYC all on her own, as Didion and Biss did, but nevertheless, like them, she often found herself lonely. Here is a difference. Lana had never *not* been lonely. Even when she was with Matthew, he rightly observed that she carried her solitude with her. Lana had never not felt invisible. Lana had never expected brief exchanges on the street to be anything but painful. Dwelling where she could continue to be lonely in the anonymous company of others was, in fact, of some comfort. If Didion was a disillusioned heroine bidding farewell to the Fair, and Biss dubious of both the protagonist and the weary narrative, Lana had never conceived of herself as a heroine of any story, let alone her own.

Didion avoids a racial reading of NYC, though twice she refers to Chinese laundries where she would break into tears. Biss is cognizant of the racialized meanings of Harlem, Washington Heights, and the outer boroughs. When she collides with another biker in Chinatown, though none of the faces that mill around her prone body are defined, no one's race named, she notes the racial markers: the ad for Asian escorts, the "reek of the fish market," the "orange bags of bok choy." Lana, who never rode a bike in the city until she met me, identifies as the non-named other in Biss's essay, possibly porting a pink plastic bag of lychees while lingering to see if the poor white girl is okay but more likely shoving her way through the crowd. A foreigner among them as well, Lana never found a community with Taiwanese Americans or Asian Americans or Taiwanese or Chinese or Asians. But in New York, for the first time in her life, she might be around, even surrounded by, people who looked like her. Even if she felt ostracized by or from them, their mere existence made her feel a little less like a freak.

On an invigorating spring day, the kind that is rare in the short-lived springtime of New York, but that the city can deliver to perfection, Matthew told Lana about a dream he'd had. In the dream Lana is leaving town, and Matthew sees her off. He then goes to her Thirteenth Street apartment and sits there indulging in the sun. He feels a figure pass by silently, cross through the apartment, and then leave. He remembers that Lana has given the woman down the hall permission to use her apartment as a shortcut. He then walks into Lana's bedroom and sees that someone is in her bed. Whipping off the covers, he discovers Lana, looking sheepish. All she says is, "I couldn't go."

Although a dream, for Lana this scenario ached with truth. During these years of living alone in the city, most days she would rather tuck herself into hiding than leave the apartment, she would rather not attend the event, she was even an intruder in her own bed. She might go days without speaking to another living being. She sometimes wished she were a plant that could thrive behind drawn shades rather than craving sunlight, one that could be nourished by isolation rather than thirsting for care. She lamented that she couldn't water herself.

Lana imagined herself as Jeanne Dielman, the eponymous character of Chantal Akerman's three-hour-and-twenty-one-minute opus, doing the dishes, cooking serviceable meals, shopping, searching for a missing button with exacting if passionless determination. She did not prostitute herself, nor did she have a son to serve, nor did she ritually make her bed, but in her fantasies a cold-blooded crime was not beyond her. Yes, she could conceive of the possibility of committing murder as Jeanne Dielman does, with as little compunction, as if it were just another item on the to-do list. I do not know this Lana but was clued into her latent sinister tendencies early on when for her birthday movie date with me she chose *Les Blessures Assassines (Murderous Maids)*, based upon an actual crime that took place in 1930s France.

In New York in the 1990s, Lana ate lima bean, potato, split pea, borscht, and mushroom barley soup with challah bread from B&H Dairy or chicken noodle, borscht, or split pea soup at Veselka. She enjoyed the challah at B&H because it was like pillows you almost wanted to sleep on rather than eat. But Veselka was better outfitted for gatherings, even before its renovation and the onslaught of yuppies. Lana and Matthew would retreat to Veselka's then dark and cramped ramshackle back room. Lana dreaded ordering here and in general. At delis where she could barely see above the high glass-encased sandwich counter, she had a hard time projecting loudly enough to be heard. New York City servers rushed about from tables to kitchen. Interrupting their hurried itinerary required a temerity she hadn't yet learned. Veselka's stalwart server was a portly woman with henna-dyed hair and a beak-shaped nose, who probably resembled someone's Ukrainian grandmother, but since Lana didn't have experience with Eastern European or even East Asian grandmothers, this didn't alleviate her trepidation.

One brisk afternoon as Lana was waiting for her stuffed cabbage with mushroom gravy, she grew chilled. The door had been left open and a stiff breeze blew her napkin off the table. Lana asked Matthew if he was cold. He was not but said, "If you're cold, why don't you close the door?" Lana surveyed the room apprehensively. Seeing no one around to be bothered, she crept forward, but as she extended her hand toward the door, she heard a voice with a Ukrainian accent say, "Miss, miss, what are you doing?!" As if withdrawing her hand from a cookie jar, Lana turned around to face the red-headed waitress. She cowered as she had when as an eight-year-old she'd stepped up onto an exhibit platform in a historic house, setting off an alarm and the rushing footsteps of a security guard. In her own alarm, child Lana had grabbed at the pant legs of someone who was not her father. Her temples hammered with shame. After the door incident Lana would have avoided Veselka forever had there been other affordable options in the neighborhood.

Pearl River Mart at 277 Canal Street, a 15,000-square foot emporium of Chinese goods, was another regular destination for Lana in the early 1990s. The original owners, Ching Yeh and Ming Yi Chen, were graduate students when they came to the U.S., he in chemistry, she in economics. They shared a Taiwanese heritage with Lana, whose father came to the U.S. as a chemist and whose mother had studied mathematics. But unlike the Chens, who were pro-China, the Lins were pro-Taiwan. Despite this political difference, of which she was then blissfully unaware, Lana was jubilant when she first roved Pearl River's crowded aisles, banked by shelves crammed with enamel-coated metallic wash basins, bamboo sushi rolling mats, butcher knives, chopsticks and chopstick rests, and queued "Chinese" pink and blue pin cushions, paper lanterns bobbing overhead. She spent hours groping plastic-wrapped pajamas and cloth shoes stacked in collapsing boxes, emerging onto the street sneezing and with blackened fingers.

But mostly she treasured the notebooks. Lana used to purchase 6.5″ x 8.25″ black notebooks with red corners and spines and off-white pages. Over time, as the notebooks grew worn, one could see that they were actually red with black paper covering the front and back, which would gradually peel away. Lining them up on her bookshelf with the year of their contents labeled in black Sharpie on their exposed spines gave her great satisfaction. Their uniformity was comforting, and they fit well into her backpack. At some point Pearl River stopped carrying them, possibly when they re-located and became much more upscale. Relying on notebooks of odd shapes and sizes gravely impacted Lana's journaling practice. More and more, she found herself leaving the apartment without anything upon which to record her thoughts. In fact, she scarcely handwrites at all anymore, to her immense disappointment. Lana was always a slow and infrequent writer, but writing has been a constant in her life.

I am given the impression that for most of the 1990s Lana Lin was either grouchy or anxious or mournful. When I arrived on the scene in 2000, all her friends, whether intimate or acquaintance, welcomed me with enthusiasm because it was well known how unhappy and downright grumpy Lana was, and it came as a tremendous relief that someone would at last act as a buffer between Lana and the world, for the world's sake as much as for Lana's.

"Most of the time I am angry," Katherine Min proclaims in her 2005 essay "Of Anger and Ambivalence." When Lana was in her mid-twenties, almost every day involved an encounter that made her angry: an Orthodox Jewish woman eyeing her as if she were trespassing in a building where they had passed each other on the staircase for over a decade, a Chinese American TV producer asking which school she attends after she has engaged him in what she believed was a conversation about her job as a college professor, a white female neighbor stepping in front of her to sign the voting roster as Lana is pulling out her ID to show a poll worker, men in subway cars squeezing her into a space half the size of the gap between their legs.

When Lana first encountered Lela Lee's Angry Little Asian Girl cartoon, it resonated with her completely. She became a proud owner of an iPhone case graced with the ALAG: "I hate people," the character stews as she slouches on a rock. That the Angry Little Asian Girl was later rebranded to Angry Little Girls makes Lana angry too, as it negates the specificity of Asian girl-hood experience and reduces it to girlhood in general.

The litany of anger is tedious and exhausting for both the one who endures it and the ones who bear witness to it. I am angry at the white men who cut in front of me at cash registers, interrupt conversations to ask me where I come from, call after me on the street with *konnichiwa*, and launch into uninvited Vietnam War or tourism stories. I am angry that my family cannot cease to comment on my short hair; that Lana and I drop our arms, mine from her shoulder, hers from my waist, when we walk in certain parts of the country; that my mother-in-law demands I fetch her purse but would never dream of asking my white brothers-in-law such a thing. We do not grow out of our anger, but if we're lucky we come to terms with it.

Once in the late 1990s, Lana heard Maxine Hong Kingston do a reading somewhere in New York City. She has no recollection of having seen Maxine Hong Kingston in person, but in her red-and-black notebook she observes that Kingston reads well, "not like a Caucasian, round and clever." It is not clear to me if Lana assessed that Caucasians read in a round and clever manner or whether this was a trait of Kingston's. "She is very tiny," writes Lana, who is herself tiny. Lana learns later that Kingston is 4'9" tall, three inches shorter than her.

In a 1991 interview, Kingston talks about creating a new autobiographical form that tells the truth about dreams, visions, and prayers, a form important to "minority people, because we're always on the brink of disappearing." I think today Kingston might use the term "people of color," who are still always on the brink of disappearing. It is predicted that white people will become the minority in the U.S. by 2050. But being in the majority or minority is not why people of color are in danger of disappearing. It is because white supremacy makes non-whites disappear regardless of numbers. Testaments to the accomplishments, crimes, crises, and romance of white people have been amply recorded. But what of the seemingly insignificant, unverifiable, imaginative minutia that composes the non-heroic vernacular of people of color? This gossamer substance that interweaves our lives fuels dream work, mythmaking, and fantasies and, as Kingston notes of women of color, keeps us alive.

On February 1, 1997, Lana remembers to say "Rabbit, rabbit" when she raises her eyelids. A friend has advised her to utter the *lapin* spell on the first of every month upon waking. She strolls down Second Avenue, reassured that it will be a lucky month, and happens upon a friend of a friend whom she has run into three times in the last week or so. The acquaintance exclaims, "You're looking really great these days, I mean, really happy. Positive energy is exuding from you. What's going on with your hair? It's really a subtle difference, but I love it." As Lana recapitulates this effusive encounter in her journal, it sounds a little overboard, but suddenly it's as if it were all true, like she really is looking good and that this is a true reflection of her inner being. Her love life is nonexistent, her current film a Rubik's Cube of impossibility, and she still has no clue how to build a career or earn more than a subsistence-level salary. Yet somehow she feels that she is spontaneously coming into her own.

Maybe it makes sense, she thinks, *that it's not connected to any of those things that I always believed make up a life. I always thought,* she writes, *that's what comes from going through cancer treatment or having someone important die—none of the life-altering things have happened to me, but gradually just living did, and maybe my own life experience has taught me who I am.*

She could not have foreseen that thirteen years later she would indeed go through cancer treatment. Cancer would come without expectation, and without any foreboding. But Lana had always borne her own cloud of disquiet like the dust perennially surrounding Pig-Pen without the Peanuts character's amiability. It was my job to dissipate that mass of unease, and as a Pig-Pen admirer, my task came with ease. Until then, New York City afforded Lana the possibility of dreaming, of floundering, of rage, of sorrow, of the anonymity to be herself while groping for who that self might be.

IV.
LANA LIN BEFORE SHE CAME TO NEW YORK

Lana Lin was born in Montreal, Canada. Although her parents gave her a Chinese name that is the sonic equivalent of "happy to be in Canada," she and her family departed her partial namesake when she was about three years old. Lana remembers the cold and the flowers of Montreal, though she may associate the French colonial city with the cold more from photographs of her swaddled in a fluffy snowsuit than from an actual memory of snow.

I once remarked offhandedly, to my unceasing regret, that Lana has no people. I am sketchy on the context, but it may have been when I heard "my people" speaking in Vietnamese on the subway. For better or worse, my identity as Vietnamese is unassailable, despite a waiter in Hà Nội complimenting me on "almost getting the accent right" at the end of my only trip to Việt Nam since my escape.

Lana laments her detachment from human belonging. Though she is trained in the critique of authenticity and sensitive to the unthinking reduction of the Americas to fifty united states, she cannot escape her conviction that she is neither authentically Taiwanese nor authentically American, given the implicit whiteness inherent in the latter. Her parents referred to themselves in their native Hokkien language as "Taiwanese people." The words they used for "American people" were equated with "white people" in Lana's mind. Her parents rarely spoke of racism, but Lana knew they were conscious of race from the way they spoke about Black people. Even with her rudimentary knowledge of the tonal language, she could pick up a note of disdain in their inflection. Lana understood that she was none of these words, but she had no words for what she was.

We have joked that a birthmark on Lana's back that looks like Saturn, or a spaceship shaped like Saturn, is unique to her species. Her alien comrades will detect her sign of Saturn, which she herself cannot see, unless positioned between two mirrors, or a smartphone and a mirror. This epidermal emblem reassures me that I can identify her from possible imposters, a concern fostered among war-torn families. When the time comes, a spaceship will land and all who bear the mark of Saturn shall be transported to where they belong, verifying the source of Lana's alienation among Earthlings. Our promise to each other is that Lana will take me with her. Somehow, I will stowaway without a Saturn entry permit, leaving my own people behind.

The first poem Lana ever memorized was Emily Dickinson's "I'm nobody! Who are you?" The poem has apparently attained some status as standard reading in elementary and junior high school curricula, and is especially appealing to Asian American girls, or so it was to both Lana Lin and Yina Liang, a sixteen-year-old student in Atlanta, Georgia who was selected to read it for the Favorite Poem Project in 1997 or 1998. From an open call, 18,000 U.S. citizens volunteered to share their favorite poems. Fifty video recitations were made, which are now housed in the Library of Congress. In her video, which includes an opening interview, Yina Liang introduces herself, sitting on the bottom bunk of a bunk bed with a red frame, an inflated red balloon behind her. The image of what we presume to be her bedroom is extraordinarily busy—anime posters and a calendar adorning the wall, pink sheets and comforter with cartoon figures draped on the top bunk, and a blue comforter decorated with horses overlaying bed sheets featuring what appears to be the Japanese pop icon hologram Hatsune Miku on the bottom bunk. A Hello Kitty figurine, a lamp with a Hawaiian lei crowning it, a couple of picture frames, and another figure peeking out from behind Hello Kitty balance on a bedside chest, next to which stands an aluminum container painted with an illustration of Santa Claus, the kind that sometimes comes filled with caramel corn, and a stuffed pink pig sitting on top of that. Although there might be a passing similarity between a high school Lana and Yina Liang—bookish Asian American teenage girls—the latter's bedroom is nothing like any of the rooms

Lana has called her own. Yina's room proudly announces her fandom and frivolity. Lana may have harbored passions, but they were seldom put on display. Even now she only sporadically places a picture on the wall.

Yina Liang is an immigrant from China. She bemoans the pressure she receives from her family and in school to be perfect. Dickinson's poem speaks to her because she yearns to be nobody. She chooses to read the poem aloud in Stone Mountain Park, her favorite place in the world, where she can breathe and not think, and just be nobody. As she recites the poem likely she does not think about the mammoth Confederate memorial that looms behind her, the carving that Stacey Abrams called for removal of in 2017 when she was a Democratic candidate for governor of Georgia. What does it mean that a Chinese American girl, lying on a blanket before what has been deemed the largest monument to white supremacy in the world, a carving that immortalizes General Lee, Jefferson Davis, and Thomas J. "Stonewall" Jackson, identifies with a white woman's paean to anonymity?

The first stanza of the 1861 version of the poem reads:

I'm Nobody! Who are you?
Are you – Nobody – too?
Then there's a pair of us!
Don't tell! they'd banish us – you know!

Who is the pair in this dichotomous scene? Dickinson goes on to commiserate with the reader against the dreary Somebody who must suffer from an admiring Bog. "Somebody" at Stone Mountain might be Ku Klux Klan Imperial Wizard W. J. Simmons and his admiring Bog of KKK Knights who held their 1915 cross burning rebirth ceremony there. "Somebody" might be Dr. Martin Luther King, who hears freedom ring from Stone Mountain. "Somebody" might also be the pastors, Black and white, leading the OneRace Movement, who signed the Atlanta Covenant at Stone Mountain in 2018 before two thousand evangelical Christians, believing in gospel-centered racial reconciliation.

Who is hailed as "Somebody" or as "Nobody" determines who is to be banished. The OneRace Movement advocates for intersection not intersectionality. They would banish difference for a gray, dreary unity. It was because of her intersectional identities that Lana felt she was Nobody and had nobody with whom to pair. But she fiercely protected her intersectionality, although she did not know it by that name, because it might make her a secret Somebody, if only to herself. How to wade through the contradictions of suspecting that the very thing that makes you distinctive within a homogenous environment is what makes you invisible? The poem pinpointed Lana's ambivalence in this contradictory position, which she could not articulate, but which settled around her as an amorphous murkiness not unlike a bog.

Deceptively simple, as most of Dickinson's poetry is, the confusion the poem elicits is enhanced through circulation of two different versions. The handwritten manuscript, accessible via an online exhibition at the Morgan Library, shows that Dickinson offered "advertise" as an alternative to "banish." Dickinson scholar Alexandra Socarides sorts out this mystery thus: "[Dickinson] invites us to think of [the variants] as possible synonyms, so that to be advertised *is to be banished*, and to be banished *is to be advertised*. . . . [S]he was thinking about the relationship between banishment and publicity." I reserve judgement on this bold interpretation. To Lana it is intriguing, suggesting more meanings that continue to elude her.

The Nobody in Dickinson's poem makes a claim on non-identity with the insistence of Yina Liang's bedroom decor, the way I did when as a child I leapt up on the divan and imitated my favorite Vietnamese opera character, announcing, "I present myself to you!" To complicate matters, Dickinson's Nobody can only disdain being Somebody in confidence with another Nobody. Lana didn't feel confident proclaiming herself to be Nobody without reassurance from another body. In the thirty-four years before finding her fellow Nobody, she lived in the hope of discovering that Somebody with whom she could be Nobody, that Somebody who would recognize her hidden mark, with whom she could escape if needed.

Much as I cathect to Dickinson's poetry, the romance of hidden genius, of the white woman sheltered from the world, is a stranglehold for young girls. Yina Liang finds comfort in what she interprets as a flight from demands for perfection. With a cadence that calls to mind Lana's mother, Liang describes Dickinson as having the ability to be "not bothered." There must be a Chinese word for the state of not being bothered about the world. Lana's mother has encouraged this worry-free attitude at her daughter's lowest moments. When Lana confronted her mother about favoring her eldest sister, Lana's mother initially dismissed the accusation, then refuted it, then in the last round of the match sighed in exasperation, "Just don't think about it, don't be bothered," apparently oblivious to the irony of enjoining the daughter into whom she had drilled the sanctity of academic achievement not to think. By *don't think* Lana's mother meant something closer to *don't worry*, which Lana admits is one of her perennial habits. Still, to equate fretting with thinking is maddening to Lana.

Both of Lana's parents grew up with a Taiwanese breed of Buddhism mixed with ancestor worship as a backdrop to daily life. They passed none of this on to Lana or her sisters, who were raised without a religion. When Lana's father reached the age of seventy-two, he had a religious epiphany. He suffered from an undetected bleeding ulcer and suddenly experienced difficulty breathing. Before or after he fainted, he made a pact with the Christian God that if his life was saved, he would believe in Him. Lana's mother accompanied her husband to their local Taiwanese Protestant church, probably initially for social purposes. Soon, singing in the choir, chanting words of salvation in communion, became a salve. Religion—she would say God—calmed the wrath that had once churned inside her when her children were young. She found peace in putting her life in God's hands.

Lana disdains her parents' Christianity as a form of obedience to a higher authority that acquiesces to injustice. But she speculates that her parents' conversion from scientists to congregants could be a belated defense against the humiliations they regularly endured as new immigrants: being asked what gas station he worked at, in the case of Lana's father, who was employed as a research chemist for twenty-six years at Standard Oil, later called Amoco, now BP, or the pain of racist, sexist, ageist treatment, in the case of Lana's mother, who was hired at Amoco as a middle-aged woman with three daughters. Mrs. Lin didn't want to think it was discrimination when she arrived at her interview and the senior chemist brushed her off with, "Oh, you're Y.C.'s wife, you're forty-six years old, why have you come here? Go home to your husband and children." According to my mother-in-law, she reassured her "superior" that she wanted to work and accepted both the snide comment and the job without overthinking it.

When Lana started kindergarten, her mother was told that her teachers were afraid Lana was "retarded." Lana's mother was dismayed because her youngest daughter could already read. The teachers had surmised that Lana was "retarded" because she did not speak, being morbidly shy at school. Lana has told me this story several times, but her mother denies it ever happened. None of her children are "retarded," she insists. "I have a sister who is retarded. Maybe Lana is confused. The housekeeper dropped my sister from a high floor to the patio. She got a fever and then couldn't count or speak very well. She was very pretty. The prettiest of us all." Lana's sisters also do not recall this incident. We can conclude that Lana's mother said something that made Lana feel "retarded," yet in this memory, external authorities deem Lana "retarded" and her mother rejects the assessment, not so much because of Lana's intelligence as because her own flesh would not be less than or other than "normal."

At school Lana rarely spoke, yet this was also the child who once stood on a picnic bench and sang "Jingle Bells" for whoever could hear her in the park, while proudly tapping her favorite red shoes, and who was known to perform a party trick where she balanced on her toes, her big toe sticking forward and all her little toes tucked under, bearing most of her weight. In certain situations, then, Lana couldn't pipe down. This was apparent the first and only time she was invited to her sisters' piano lessons. Lana's Midwestern suburban life was very sheltered, and she was not exposed to many environments except her house, her school, and the Naperville Public Library. Brimming with excitement, Lana entered the piano teacher's sitting room. As her middle sister, Cynthia, trotted down the hall for her lesson, Lana gazed around, unable to focus on anything because there was so much to see. This room was decorated—someone had put things out to be seen, and had placed them in a particular, loving manner—which made it a novelty for her.

In her family home, things were out because they were needed or were lying around because they were no longer needed. Things were everywhere but nothing was placed purposefully, nor was anything displayed simply to be seen. The only objects Lana recalls that were not expressly functional were a collection of miniature glass animals that her mother kept on her dresser. This vitreous compendium bewitched Lana because it was so unlike anything else her family owned. It hinted at another life her mother led as a young woman, one who might accumulate things for pleasure. Lana was fond of stroking the animals because of their soothing polish. She put her eye up to them, so close that her lashes would brush the surface and she could squint through their translucent interiors. There was a doe and a fawn or two that may have been connected by a tiny chain. Lana is baffled that she cannot remember the others, since at the time she marveled at them. Was there a lion, a bear, a giraffe? There must have been a rabbit, and possibly a small dog with wavy hair, but the only one she is certain of to any degree is the deer. That must have been her favorite. Lana's mother has forgotten where she put them, although she knows that she has not thrown them away. She recollects a horse, zebra, duckling, chicken or hen, and something with a long neck. She is confident that the menagerie did not include a cow or a pig, because even though she was born in the year of the pig, she is not partial to them.

Though I have never seen my mother-in-law's collection, Lana's description reminds me of a glass curio cabinet that my parents had in Sài Gòn. It contained crystal stemware, miniatures that my dad inherited, a ceramic wise man, and a wooden horse carriage that tempted me to touch it. The cabinet's lock prevented me from acting on my desires, and I would ogle the fragile captives for what seemed like hours. My parents had learned from an earlier incident that mere threats were not enough to deter my destructive instincts. When they'd purchased a multicolored modern credenza, I'd taken a knife to its facade, though thankfully not down its entire length. My distressed parents asked if I was the culprit, and I readily admitted to what I did not conceive of as a crime. I'd had an irrepressible urge to soften the cupboard's edge, and organic materials seduced me, especially wood.

Held in a hexagonal bookcase in her friend's house before they were gifted to her, my mother-in-law's collectibles were also protected behind glass, as were the tchotchkes in the piano teacher's sitting room. Lana's oldest sister, JuPong, who went by her Anglicized name, Polly, at the time, pointed out the busts of famous composers, naming them: Bach, Beethoven, Brahms. Lana pranced around the room, bubbling with glee. She doesn't remember what she was yammering about when Mrs. May flung open the door and told Lana that if she couldn't keep quiet, she would have to leave. Lana felt the blood flooding her cheeks, and then rushing away. She bolted herself to a chair and silenced herself for the next forty-five minutes, scarcely daring to look up from her flaming palms. Cynthia complained afterwards that Lana was no fun during Polly's lesson.

This dramatic physical reaction to overstepping her welcome, for being heard instead of only seen, or even seen when she should not be visible at all, has plagued Lana, at parties, in cafeterias, in common spaces meant for social relaxation yet anxiety-inducing for her. Making herself as quiet, small, and as close to invisible as possible had long been her goal. The waitress at Veselka reignited Lana's shame of reaching beyond herself.

But now and then when life rushes too explosively for her to be peremptorily restrained, Lana can be caught out of her shell. For those few people with whom she feels comfortable enough to emerge, unprotected, unreserved, she resembles that uncontainable child before reprimand. This is the Lana I live with on most days, one that would surprise many who have come to expect from her meek submission or stern sobriety.

Lana took piano lessons with a different teacher because she wasn't good enough for her sisters' instructor, which made the tall, dark-haired Mrs. May a figure of mystery and veneration. One needed to audition for Mrs. May, who was strict and demanding, probably not unlike my mom as a schoolteacher. Lana's piano teacher, by contrast, was gentle and encouraging. Mrs. Weeks, warm and red-haired, flattered Lana, praising her talent. For that reason, Lana was convinced that Mrs. May was the better teacher whose opinion should be more highly valued.

The mnemonic phrases that many children use to learn how to read music are Every Good Boy Does Fine for the E, G, B, D, and F on the treble clef and Good Boys Do Fine Always for the G, B, D, F, and A on the bass clef. These phrases were soldered to Lana's brain, and in thirty-seven years of not playing the piano they have continued to influence many of her activities. Even as a ten-year-old, it occurred to Lana that she fit nowhere in these mantras. What does every good girl do? Not fine, surely. Good girls do fine never, it would seem. Yet being a good girl was all that Lana ever sought or was instructed to be.

The stories Lana was told as a child confirmed the futility of her actions. *Tikki Tikki Tembo* was a story that gave Lana unending entertainment because her oldest sister read it with such zeal. Supposedly based on Chinese folklore, it is likely based on a Japanese tale, *Jugemu*, and was written by Arlene Mosel, a librarian from Cleveland, Ohio. It is the tale of two "Chinese" brothers, Tikki Tikki Tembo-no Sa Rembo-chari Bari Ruchi-pip Peri Pembo, which meant, in this nonsense language, "the most wonderful thing in the whole wide world," and his younger brother, Chang, meaning "little or nothing." Polly read the older brother's impossibly long name like she was sprinting, inhaling with exaggeration, articulating the tongue-twisting name in a single breath and ending up panting. This invariably cracked up Lana and Cynthia. Lana was enchanted by this story. She took little notice of the fact that not only were there no daughters in it, there were only two siblings. It felt familiar to her not to directly identify with characters or stories, which may partially explain how she could enjoy a racist, sexist fable so much.

In the 1970s, *Tikki Tikki Tembo* and *The Seven Chinese Brothers* by Margaret Mahy were the only children's books that Lana could check out of the library that had "Asian" characters. If Lana wanted to identify with a character, she did so obliquely, willfully misidentifying with characters she knew were white but at least had dark hair: the Louis Darling depiction of Ramona the Pest, for example, or Marcie in *Peanuts*. Even now, Lana feels betrayed by the updates of Ramona and Marcie in which their original black hair is colored in as brunette.

The 1976 Summer Olympics took place in the city of Lana's birth. She was enthralled by Nadia Comăneci whose brunette ponytail looked black on her family's black-and-white TV. Lana could neither root for Asian Americans nor Asians from the country of her heritage. Taiwan-based athletes boycotted the games, having been denied official representation as the Republic of China. Since 1984 Taiwan has competed under the name "Chinese Taipei," which is as nonsensical as Tikki Tikki Tembo. "Chinese" indicates a nationality or descendent or inhabitant of China and "Taipei" a city, but the fabricated moniker points to no known nation. As Chris Horton quips in the *New York Times*, it would be like requiring the U.S. to call itself "British Washington" as a condition of participating in a major international event. Even that isn't quite analogous. It would be more like "British Washington, D.C.," which possibly Horton rejected because it is rhythmically clunky, but its ungainliness makes it an even more fitting comparison.

On occasion, the Lins gathered in front of the television to watch Chinese acrobats and performers. Months in advance Lana's parents were informed by friends when PBS would air special cultural programs. For *The White-Haired Girl*, the ballet version of the Communist revolutionary opera, Lana's mother prepared something special, like custard puffs or meat-filled pockets made from Jiffy pie crust mix, kind of a Chinese empanada. Or maybe it was meatballs rolled in rice that Lana would stab with a chopstick and chomp on while galloping around the living room. It was probably not the white almond Jell-O that Lana strained through her teeth, mushing against her cheeks, because Jell-O was a summer treat and such TV events tended to happen during the winter holiday months.

Lana understood that it wouldn't behoove her to emulate the White-Haired Girl, whose hair turned white for a reason, even though the brave and beautiful heroine triumphs in the end, as one would expect of propaganda. Years of abuse and slave labor is too high a price to pay for being worshipped as a goddess. Lana's attention flagged during the tedious scenes of revolutionary fervor but keyed in on moments when the White-Haired Girl, luminously garbed in white, displayed her bravura talent. The White-Haired Girl's exceptionalism ironically undermines the ballet's communist message, and despite joining the ranks of her comrades in the finale, she remains marked by her white hair. Lana gleaned from the ballet that women needed to undergo extreme hardship so that their common invisibility would be transformed into visibility. With her shimmering tresses, the White-Haired Girl advertised herself as Somebody, but the narrative claimed her to be Nobody. She was of the people, yet her sign of Saturn distinguished her from her "tribe."

Lana's parents did not read her bedtime stories when she was a child, but there was one set of stories that her father read to her when she was in middle school because they were written in Chinese, which she never learned to read. Lana was fascinated with the Chinese books her parents owned because they opened backwards. She used to lie on her parents' bed, flipping to the pictures in the slim books, which were more like magazines. This series of morality tales, Lana now knows, are the twenty-four paragons or exemplars of filial piety written by

Guo Jujing during the Yuan Dynasty. A handful are tucked into her bookshelf at present although she still cannot read them herself. The illustrations jog her memory. The story that Lana requested most frequently was "Tears that Brought Bamboo-shoots from the Frozen Earth: Meng Zong" or "He Wept Till the Bamboo Sprouted (Mèng Zōng)" wherein a boy who needs to find bamboo for his dying mother in winter enters a grove and weeps bitter tears since bamboo typically cannot grow in such cold. Heaven and earth take pity on the obedient son, and from his tears sprout tender stalks. He collects the shoots and makes a curative soup for his mother.

Guilt welled up in Lana as she listened to these tales of self-lessness; surely she was remiss in her own filial duties. One of the parables tells of a man who sold himself into servitude to pay for a proper burial for his father. Another describes a boy who allows mosquitoes to bite him so they do not disturb his parents' sleep. Lana could not imagine offering her breast for her mother-in-law to suckle, if she could ever produce breast milk, which she could also not imagine even before she had a breast removed due to cancer. The comic book-style drawing of "She Suckled Her Mother-in-Law (Madam Cui)" or "Never Tiring of Feeding Milk to Her Mother-In-Law: Lady Tang" off-sets what might appear lewd in a photograph: a beautiful and sad woman cradles her own breast, from which a feeble gray-haired woman feeds, while a beseeching boy, no doubt the one for whom the milk was lactated, kneels on the floor weeping and stretching up toward the withholding woman.

The Chinese government updated the classic text in 2012 to "The New Twenty-Four Paragons of Filial Piety," urging off-spring to take their aging parents on vacation frequently, throw them a birthday party, and listen to their stories from the past. Straining under the effects of globalization, modern-day Chinese are apparently becoming increasingly alienated from their ancestral bonds, bonds that Lana never experienced. From Lana's view, when her parents immigrated to Canada, they made a radical break. Over the years her father would muse about retiring in Taiwan, but as his retirement age approached it was clear that the mythic Taiwan of his youth no longer existed, and that he was more than content with the life he had built in the U.S.

Taiwan was shrouded in mystery to Lana, and the family members who resided there were more like characters in a novel she hadn't and could not read. Infrequently she would hear, either late at night or early in the morning, her parents shouting in Taiwanese at their black rotary phone, which was attached to the kitchen wall, its unruly cord refusing to disentangle. On occasion a Taiwanese relative or friend would stop by and a mammoth suitcase would be stuffed with Silkience or Finesse shampoo, among other items Lana can't remember. She asked her sister, "Don't they have shampoo in Taiwan?" and was told, "Yes, but not the nice kind." Lana first visited Taiwan when she was seventeen. She can count the number of times she has visited on one hand. It has always felt like a foreign country to her, one with which she possesses a strange, estranged connection, as if she were an adopted child meeting her biological parent in adulthood.

Lana never got to know her grandparents. She never met her maternal grandfather. Only once was she in the presence of her maternal grandmother. It felt like a scene from a movie. Even as it was happening, Lana felt like she was standing outside of it, watching. And now the scene is only dimly visible through a ragged hole torn in the fabric of her memory. Perhaps this is because, as both of Lana's sisters attest, the room they entered was dark and smoky, either from incense or from her grandmother's cigarettes or both. An old woman with dyed black hair sits hunched over on a bed. Lana's sister remembers an ornate bedframe, the kind that is almost like a little room unto itself. The stranger speaks in low tones. Probably their mother had gone in before them. Possibly the granddaughters were told they should greet their grandmother. Lana likely retorted that she didn't know how. Someone may have urged, "Just say, *A ma* (grandma) and your name."

Polly, who would have been called JuPong or the more affectionate A Pong in her homeland, would have spoken first because she was the eldest and could speak Taiwanese, or at least Taiwanese was her first language. A Pong was renowned in the Lin family for being able to recite everyone's names in the genealogy and their relation to her, a feat that is often used to assess the acuity of children, and forever functions as a barometer of their intelligence or lack thereof. Lana was undoubtedly consumed with anxiety about how to address her grandmother and how to pronounce her own name in Taiwanese. Her uneasiness has extinguished her memories of the first and only time she set eyes on her maternal grandmother. She presumes that at some point her mother's mother passed away, although neither she nor her mother attended the funeral.

Lana's paternal grandparents are more dimensional, although not by much. Her father's father exuded the demeanor of a proud, somewhat tyrannical patriarch. Her father's mother possessed the kind of toughness you would expect from a rural Taiwanese woman who reared nine children while tending to a dwelling with a dirt floor, slaughtering pigs, harvesting potato leaves, and applying medicinal remedies, among innumerable other chores. During the Japanese occupation, when speaking let alone reading Chinese was forbidden, she recited the Thousand-Character Classic, a poem used to teach Chinese ideograms to children, while she cooked. She was determined that her eldest son be able to wield the power of language in the soon-to-be new rulers' tongue. This iron-willed woman must have resembled my own grandmother. When we visited my eighty-year-old grandmother in Bến Tre and Lana offered to wash the dishes after dinner, the host would have none of that and pushed her guest, who was squatting next to her, away from the dishes with one bony index finger, toppling Lana over.

Because Lana's grandparents could not get along, in Lana's junior or senior year of high school her father invited his mother to join him in the U.S. Unlike neighboring suburbs, Naperville allowed Chinese to become homeowners, but the residents were overwhelmingly white and had no idea where or what Taiwan was. Huntington Estates, the subdivision where the Lins resided, was like a standing army, vinyl-wrapped enclosures lined up with their identically mowed lawns and sealed garages. This drab, organized existence starkly contrasted the chaos of Lana's grandmother's ancestral home. People did not congregate outside. Street vendors did not ride by hawking their wares. Roosters' cries did not disrupt the sleepy afternoon. It was a lonely and sterile existence for Lana, but at least it was the only one she had known.

I, too, was displaced from a hot climate teeming with wildlife and extended family to a frigid and foreign atmosphere, so I sympathize with the violence of such a rift. Lana's grandmother would rustle through the uninviting and unpeopled rooms like a ghost, an unsettled apparition, not knowing where to go or what to do. What was there to do for a seventy-year-old woman who could not speak English and didn't know how to drive, whose eldest son, the pride of her village, was busy at work all day, whose daughter-in-law was an uncompromising woman who bristled with unspoken rage, and whose only granddaughter still in the house could not speak her language and was born into a culture alien to her?

Since she was a child, Lana had been told her hands looked weathered and beaten like an old peasant woman's. How had she inherited her grandmother's cured leather hands, Lana wondered, without having endured hard labor? Her grandmother's enlarged knuckles could cradle uncooked rice in stiff bamboo leaves, wrapping it deftly without spilling a single grain. When Lana tried the same trick, she sent the slippery pellets scattering all over the linoleum floor.

Staring at her disapprovingly, Lana's Taiwanese relatives would ask with alarm, in Taiwanese, "What's wrong with the color of her skin?" They suspected Burger King was the culprit. Though she could not cross whatever psychological and linguistic barrier barred her from uttering even broken Taiwanese, she could comprehend it in fragments. And she resented being talked about as if she were not present, which encouraged her habit of taking internal flight whenever possible. But they might have been onto something about the ill effects of U.S. or suburban living. Life itself seemed to drain from her grandmother, who grew colorless and mute. Eventually the wizened woman returned to her home in Taiwan. Lana and her family would travel there to join the entire village in mourning the matriarch at her funeral, to the tune of Buddhist chants and a brass band.

During her adolescence, Lana began to notice that each member of the Lin clan grew increasingly isolated, suspended in their own discontented bubbles. But this isn't the right analogy, because bubbles suggest lightness, whereas this period of Lana's life was burdened with heaviness, constriction, the feeling of not being able to breathe. Lana's mother was mired in a depression she could not name. She had earned a master's degree in mathematics, having been admitted into the second-best university in Taiwan. There is no debate about the relative merits of competing universities in Taiwan. They are incontrovertibly ranked. Lana's father attended the top university. For a woman to gain entry into the second-best university was a very high achievement. Housekeeping and raising children were neither her strengths nor her ambitions.

Before she was hired as an analytical technician at Amoco, Lana's mother worked at a data center balancing the books for several banks. Human Resources called her in after three months on the job and told her that they could no longer use her because her boss said she didn't fit in with their group. "She doesn't talk to anyone," he had explained. The office didn't know how to handle the situation. It turns out they couldn't fire her outright because there weren't any problems with her work. They could only pressure her to quit, or this is what I have gathered from her digressive, sometimes contradictory anecdotes.

Mrs. Lin's colleagues spent their lunches and breaks busily gossiping and would complain in front of her: "I hate these

Asian people because their kids all go to Harvard, MIT, and Yale. They're going to take over the country." They literally said things that now sound like clichés or like skits parodying racists that one might see on *Saturday Night Live.*

Lana's mother had nothing to say to these people. "They looked down on me," she imparted to me with chagrin. "But they couldn't look down on my work."

When she was in high school, Lana was often alone in the house with her mother. Her sisters had left for college. Her father was at work. One afternoon, it might have been 1983 or '84, Lana was lying on the couch, pretending to do her algebra homework, and her mother was storming around in the kitchen banging pots and pans, as she was wont to do. Lana didn't know what her mother was upset about. It might have been because the place was a mess, which it always was because her mother tended to be the only person in the house who cleaned, and because rather than requesting that her husband and kids help with the chores, she would yell and rampage so that everyone dispersed into their own protective cocoons. Lana's father, the master of disregard, would disappear into his garden or a newspaper or somewhere else. Once, out of frustration, Polly complained, "Mom, if you're upset because no one helps you around the house, you could ask us to." Lana has no recollection of how her mother reacted. She may have scoffed and gone off in a huff. Or maybe she murmured something under her breath. In any case, in the years of venomous eruptions, Lana only remembers Polly voicing a response once. No one else dared or cared to.

This day, Lana's mother burst into the "family" room holding a meat cleaver to her throat, shouting, "I want to die. I am going to kill myself!" Lana steeled herself, taking care that she did not look up as her mother wailed. She was well practiced in this strategy of self-defense. She said to herself, *Do you think I want to live? I didn't ask to be born. You did that to me. What do you expect me to do about your suffering?* Lana did not say a word to her mother, did not even acknowledge her presence. She turned herself into stone and eventually went up to her bedroom, both proud and ashamed of her cold heartedness. She never discussed what happened with her mother, nor with anyone else, until she confided in me. She continued to attend high school, which she despised, also wishing she could die, but holding out for an escape from her family and the suburbs, which she considered a desert that couldn't nourish life. She waited for the opportunity to come to life elsewhere, to become who she might be.

Apparently, such scenes of melodrama are not uncommon for those of Chinese and Taiwanese lineage, if we can believe opera, literature, cinema, legend. One of the perennial battles Lana's grandparents were embroiled in ended with a butcher knife landing perilously close to her grandmother's head. Listening to Amy Tan narrate how her mother took a meat cleaver to her out of disapproval of Amy's boyfriend, Lana recognized something of her own family dynamic. Amy Tan's mother often threatened suicide to join her own mother who had died from an opium overdose. Like Jing-Mei in Tan's *The Joy Luck Club*, Lana's mother had half-sisters of whom Lana knows nothing except that there were four. Unlike in Tan's novel, they were not left on the side of the road during wartime. Or, they might have been, but Lana has no knowledge of it.

The war story that Lana's mother tells is of an air raid that occurred while she was in school. She recalls running home as bombs dropped around her younger brother and older sister, the one who suffered brain damage and who could only sing and run. When they reached the gate of the factory that their mother owned, they cried out. Their mother grabbed all her children as a hen who has spotted a hawk circling in the sky swaddles her chicks under her wing and protects them from harm. She led them to the kitchen where she shoved them under her sizeable sink. All four children—the youngest just a baby not in school yet—squeezed together, waiting in terror for the bombing to subside. When it did, Lana's grandmother called the police to remove the bomb that had landed in their front yard. For Lana's mother, this tale exemplifies a mother's devotion to her children.

My mother-in-law has nothing but praise for her own mother. Lana sniffs repression in her mother's rapturous idealization. Another pivotal moment that secured Lana's mother's fierce attachment to her own mother took place when Lana's mother was five years old. Her father's best friend was a man named Chen. Uncle and Auntie Chen came over to their house because her father, who had sired many girls, had agreed to give one of them to the Chens, who had none. As is the custom in Taiwan, Lana's mother, who was called See Ze, her Japanese name, refers to all her relatives in terms of their rank and relation to her. See Ze was sitting with her half-sister #2 at the door of the tatami room where they could listen to everything that transpired. See Ze's mother cajoled, "Please take See Ze. I promise you; you won't have made the wrong decision. She is very good and very smart."

Lana's mother bolted herself to the mat, shocked. She glowered at the Chens, her face dark. Unsmiling and silent, she inwardly fumed, "Don't touch me." See Ze's older sister, the one who could only sing and run but was very pretty, the prettiest of them all, overheard voices and dashed into the room.

"Take me!" she cried. "I'd like to go with you." Turning to the servant, she urged, "Pack my bag. I'll go with them." The Chens looked from one girl to the next and escorted the charming one to their home.

As soon as they stepped off the property, See Ze's biological aunt protested, "What is wrong with you?! Why did you let them take your child?"

See Ze's mother replied with a Taiwanese expression that the palm of your hand belongs to your body, but when you turn it to the backside, it is also part of your body. Either way, it's your hand. "Look at See Ze. Look how ugly she is. Look how she hates people. I know this girl will protect herself. The older one will be back in not more than two days," she predicted. "They will realize she has a problem in her head and send her back."

In not more than two days, See Ze's pretty sister returned. "She doesn't remember anything," Lana's mother reflects. "But I remember everything." When See Ze went to high school, she met the Chen's adopted daughter who attended the same school.

While my mother-in-law lauds her own mother's wisdom, Lana and I have noticed that she sneaks in her aunt's indignation. See Ze could never question her mother's methods, but her aunt, even as foil, may be the alter ego my mother-in-law could never be, the one who recognizes cruelty even if it comes under the guise of maternal care. Though my mother-in-law has no truck with psychoanalysis, her final appraisal that she remembers everything confirms Freud's truism that nothing in the unconscious ever dies.

In a file folder labeled "Stories," I turn up two yellowing pages dated March 20, 1991, which Lana typed on the first typewriter she ever bought, a Panasonic electric with a memory function:

My mother did not tell me stories. She did not have the capacity for it. She resisted the impulse to comfort and never read bedtime stories aloud. The sound of her voice was neither song nor story, but fury in a language I do not know.

My mother did not tell me stories. She did not have the stomach for it. Her stomach was filled with pigs' feet and roosters' neck. She served a tasty roast duck, but she had no time for storytelling.

What has she left behind to do the telling? Woolen skirts and Skippy jars. They were poor, my parents when they first arrived in Canada. All they could afford was peanut butter and ground fish sandwiches. And the bread was Wonder white. There I was, a newborn laid to rest next to a licked-clean Skippy jar that was just about as big as my head. I don't remember it, but I have the photo to prove it. It's the only one. Film was a luxury item.

I'm rummaging in boxes jammed with permanently wrinkled clothing. My fingers land upon two finely tailored wool skirts. I hold off my dismay and step into one. My thighs will barely fit through it.

I am reminded of a film I saw in grade school about metamorphosis. The bloody birth of an infant kangaroo, a wet bud of slime lost in the fur of its mother's pouch; baby tadpoles swimming off into murky streams to become warty, belching frogs.

I glimpse an inconceivable chasm between birth and middle age, between refined wool skirts and polyester stretch pants. Cinching a twenty-one-inch band around my girth, I experience my mother's waist when my head was the size of a Skippy jar.

My mother was an excellent seamstress. When I was in grade school, she cut her own patterns—flared pants, flowered dresses that hung to the floor. Mother and child, cut apart at creation, sewn together again. When did the rips take place? We never got to patching things up between us. She stopped making my clothes when I got old enough to dislike them.

Now I remember one story my mother told me. My parents were newly married, burdened with an infant, and immigrants in a giant nation covered with snow. My father brought home a meager salary paid in cash. My mother didn't trust banks. She would stash the bills in the drawer of a portable wardrobe that folded into a heavy-duty chest. Her family agreed it was the only thing sturdy enough to survive the journey. She had mistakenly packed only fancy dresses and pleated skirts. She did not realize how much housekeeping there would be to do.

It was Friday and my father had just been paid. My mother needed to buy groceries for the weekend. She knew she shouldn't leave the baby alone, but she just had to run to the corner to buy some milk. She left the apartment for fifteen, maybe twenty minutes. When she returned the skirt that she had laid on the bed was covered with vomit. That night she had to hand wash it several times to get rid of the putrid smell.

It's interesting that Lana writes this autofiction as if her mother were dead and her sisters never existed. But there are some truthful elements in the story. Every time her mother took out a package of the dried fish her daughters loved, she reminded her youngest to chew carefully and not eat too much because once she gorged on the salty snack and threw up. It is also true that when she was young, Lana's mother had a slender waist, impeccably tailored wool skirts, and that she left baby Lana home alone at some point.

On an undated sheet of paper in a file labeled "Writing—Past Years," Lana handwrites:

The blonde girl from down the street appeared in our yard.

Would you like to play with me?

I stare at her blankly.

My mom bought me a new Barbie with hair that you can curl.

I stared at her still.

Don't you like Barbies? I have ten, now eleven with this new one.

I edge toward the door.

You can borrow Angie. She's not a real Barbie, but she's more like you. She has brown hair like you and is short like you. You can be Barbie's best friend.

I wonder if I could be Ken.

What are you retarded or something? I don't want to play with you anyway.

The next day I open the screen door to see that someone had cut off all the heads of the tulips that flanked the house. The guillotined flowers still haunt me.

Though she does not reveal it in this parley, Lana did own a Barbie, maybe two. Every year the Lin family would attend Amoco's annual Christmas party, the highlight of which, to Lana, was when each child could select a gift. The presents were grouped by gender and age, so, predictably, boys ripped open boxes containing trucks and rockets, and girls unwrapped dolls and baking sets. Nevertheless, Lana looked forward to the festivities because until she and her sisters were old enough to exchange presents themselves, the company's gift was the only one they would receive save for their birthdays.

Lana amassed a bevy of dolls, many of which she inherited, and none of which remotely resembled her. To her mind, a panda would come closer. She felt more in common with this nearly extinct species than with "Oriental" dolls, which aroused no sympathy in her. One year for her birthday she insisted on dragging the entire family from toy store to department store in search of a stuffed version of this endangered creature from China, a place to which she had never journeyed yet felt an obscure connection. The beast's pathos and passivity appealed to her, its unique combination of fragility and enormity, what literary theorist Eve Kosofsky Sedgwick might call its "queer chunkiness." Pandas are often described, like the Chinese, as being inscrutable. Lana, too, felt herself an inscrutable object when her Taiwanese relatives pondered aloud why her skin "looked like that," and when white strangers would ask her, "What are you?" Eventually, she did wind up with a stiff four-legged panda whose limbs were movable yet inflexible, and which remained resolutely unhuggable.

At school Lana and her friend Patty sped through their worksheets together, sharing answers and making fun of them. Patty had sandy brown hair and freckles. She was one of the few kids in school who Lana thought was smart and funny, and, even more astonishingly to Lana, she thought Lana was smart and funny as well. Or at least Lana thought Patty thought she was smart, which gave Lana the chance to be funny, because she could only be funny in the company of people with whom she felt comfortable, and she could only be comfortable with people who thought she was smart.

At some point, one of Lana's sisters told her that if someone was really your best friend, they could prove it by holding onto a special object for an entire day. The task bears a resemblance to the parenthood test in which teenagers are asked to caretake an egg for a week. But in this case, it didn't matter what the object was; in fact, the more pedestrian, the better. The act of protecting a seemingly worthless object was what mattered, rather than the object itself. Lana selected a clip that she had picked up on the street. In retrospect she thinks it was the kind of clip that might be on a dog leash. Patty must have furnished something in exchange, though Lana retains no memory of what it was. It was easy for Lana to cleave to things she cared about, and to keep the talisman Patty must have given her took so little effort she had no need to bind it to memory. I can confirm that Lana has trouble holding onto memories, but she clings to objects for which she sometimes forgets the meaning. Boxes filled and stashed away with items collected but not necessarily recollected.

Patty was popular and Lana was not. Some of Patty's gang of girlfriends found out about the silly game that she and Lana were playing. They were jealous. They distracted her. Come the end of the day Patty could not find Lana's gift.

"But we can still be friends, can't we? Just not *best* friends." She offered to buy Lana a new clip, or whatever it was.

Lana was crushed but downplayed her devastation. *It was no big deal. Of course, they could be friends, even best friends.* "I don't even know what it was," she mumbled, affecting nonchalance. "I just picked it up off the street on my way to school."

During summer vacation, Lana's sisters enjoyed bike riding, and, determined not to be left behind, Lana would join them, eager to practice new tricks on the jungle gym sets at the elementary school playground that was often their destination. The route to the playground concluded with a concrete ramp for cycles and wheelchairs alongside concrete stairs. The proximity between the ramp and the steps terrified Lana. She always pictured herself taking a nosedive into the stairs, which inevitably, one day, she did. As she approached the ramp, her front wheel wiggled uncontrollably, and she gripped her handlebars until her knuckles turned white, throwing herself off balance onto the stairs and gouging the right side of her chest. When she collected herself and her bike, she noticed blood on her T-shirt. She raised it for her sister to take a peek, and Polly bellowed, "Don't be scared, but I can see the bone!" At home, their mother slathered on her cure-all, Mentholatum, which Lana always believed caused excessive scarring. When Lana was to have a mastectomy on the same side as her biking injury, she asked the surgeon if he could make the incision at the site of her scar. He just stared at her, unmoved by Lana's bid to make a present injury cover over a past wound.

These unrelated events reverberate against each other in Lana's mind. Lana gives an object to a loved one in hopes that it will secure a bond of affection. The clip is lost rather than secured. Lana suffers a blow that she interprets as punishment for taking a risk, for extending herself beyond the safe confines of her interior life. The opportunity for a fresh scar to dissolve a former one is refused. A scar can act like a screen memory, masking a submerged trauma. Lana sought to press the surgeon to do what even the psychoanalyst cannot, to control the palimpsest of embodied memory. I can relate both to the unruliness of memory and to the persistence of a scar's meaning. We both have had biking accidents that have inscribed themselves onto our flesh.

A gift may impose a burden upon the recipient, if it is given on condition that one performs as dutiful subject, as proper girl or boy, as best friend. Lana didn't consider the item exactly a gift, or if it was, it was conditional, and so was it a gift or was it poison?

Lana feels herself incapable of loving without being loved in equal measure. She cannot compass devotion without return. At the same time Lana believes love cannot call itself love if it is not beyond measure. I suspect she has always harbored this expectation, though she never believed it would be fulfilled.

Lana Lin associates her time before she came to New York with the image of flowers whose blossoms have been amputated. She collapses herself into the figure of horrified onlooker, the cause of violence and its recipient. If she had not yearned to be held as equal in a pair, a pair of Somebodies, or better, Nobodies, she would not have invited betrayal and loss. Though the characters are different, the story feels the same.

She severed the heads of every tulip
In the plot, leaving only
Stems craning skyward
Beckoning, forlorn, alien

V.
2001–2019

At 8:51 A.M. the temperature was 81 degrees in New York City. Lana was in her second year of teaching full time at the City College of New York. It was not one of her teaching days, so she woke up late. The sun was streaming into her compact east-facing apartment as it always did because Lana never invested in window coverings until I suggested the novel idea of blinds. This was when I became aware that most walls in old New York City buildings are made of concrete, which offers the benefit of muffling the sound between apartments but is extremely resistant to drilling. I lost countless drill bits to these impenetrable walls. But until the momentous occasion of my installing blinds, the sun would beat down on the paint-caked, grimy windowsills and worn, blackened wood floors, and Lana would simply endure the heat or move aside. She treated windows as if they were two-way mirrors; she could peer out into the urban landscape but was oblivious to those who might return her gaze. She felt she was magically protected from onlookers, perhaps by being on the fifth floor, the other buildings too far away, or she simply surmised that other New Yorkers would be as incurious about her private life as she was about theirs.

Lana automatically turned on the radio every morning, flipping the switch on her boom box, which was reliably tuned to WNYC AM 820. The WNYC studios were two blocks away from the World Trade Center. On air that morning, someone repeatedly remarked upon how low the plane was flying. He was on the twenty-sixth floor of the Manhattan Municipal Building. The first plane struck the North Tower at 8:46 A.M. By 9:03 A.M. two commercial jets had barreled through the iconic structures, and suspicion grew that "foul play" was involved. But the newscasters did not know how many people had been hurt or, as they said, "even killed."

Lana can't remember if Matthew phoned her or if she called him, but they met up. They trudged through the East Village, dazed and unnerved, sirens accompanying them like the soundtrack to a disaster/science fiction/horror movie. The screeching reached a pitch that she had never experienced before and did not relent for at least the next twelve hours, or was it twenty-four, or was it days?

Matthew and Lana sat outside St. Mark's Church, stunned, as an endless procession of emergency vehicles followed one after another, and wondered if they were coming from upstate New York, possibly beyond, maybe even Canada, though they would find out later that the air space over the U.S. had been shut down, and planes were grounded in Canada. Lana did not witness in person the dust- and soot-coated escapees nor the nearby pedestrians nor the first or second responders, which made the images she viewed on her television seem that much closer to *Night of the Living Dead.*

Lana did not know financial analysts, or janitors, or door-men, or mailroom workers, or servers or staff at Windows on the World, or anyone who worked at or had the misfortune to be in the World Trade Towers that day. She did not know Michael Richards, the artist who had a studio on the 92nd floor of the North Tower as part of the Lower Manhattan Cultural Council (LMCC) World Views program. An acquaintance of hers was desperately calling around and writing emails to find out if anyone had heard from him.

Aside from attending the LMCC open studios that occurred in the late 1990s, Lana did not have many reasons to be at the World Trade Center. Her image of the emblematic modernist buildings derived mostly from movies, even her own. In 1996, Lana took a 16 mm Bolex camera on board the Staten Island ferry and, as it pulled away from shore, tilted up from the trail of foamy water to catch the Twin Towers in her lens. The black-and-white footage appears in her 1997 featurette adapting the life of writer Jane Bowles, who lived on Staten Island in 1938 with her better-known husband Paul Bowles before they both became expatriates in Tangier. The biofiction screens infre-quently, but the last time it was projected, in a cramped, sweaty backroom of a London gallery, Lana was startled by the grainy wraiths that flickered up from the East River, casting a nostalgic spell upon the film.

From a documentary, Lana later learned that it was an Asian American flight attendant, Betty Ong, who notified the American Airlines Reservations Desk that a hijacking might be happening. The documentary includes the recording. With an impressively resolute tone, Ong reports that the cockpit is not answering. Someone has been stabbed in business class, and no one can breathe. The flight attendant suspects someone has mace. She is made to reiterate this several times as the voices on the other end of the line repeatedly ask her what seat she is in. She says that their #1 has been stabbed as well as their #5. There is a protracted pause and she pleads, "Hello?" The man on the other end replies that he is taking it all down, and of course they are recording this. On Ong's eighth and ninth repetition of the word "stabbed," her voice wavers slightly.

Alarming news can have the opposite effect than alarm. It is as if our defenses muffle our ears. Several people were patched into Betty Ong's alarming Airfone call, each of whom seems to take some time to absorb the gravity of the situation. Likewise, the air traffic communications proceeded with apparent confusion, traveling over speed bumps of disbelief. The Federal Aviation Administration's Boston Center contacted New York Air National Guard Tech. Sergeant Jeremy Powell, who inquires: "Is this real world or exercise?"

A firm response: "No, this is not an exercise, not a test."

As of midday September 12, the last survivor, of only twelve, was pulled from the rubble. Over the next few days, Lana walked tentatively past FDNY Ladder 3 and Battalion 6, the fire station on Thirteenth Street between Third and Fourth Avenues, humbled by the shrines to those who'd perished in the line of duty 136 years to the day after the ladder company was established. Scanned photographs of the missing fluttered from every fence and post, papered the exterior walls of buildings, and peered through store windows. Anti-war protests and vigils were held in Union Square Park amid the amassed ribbons, candles, flowers, flags, and photographs of lost loved ones.

While participating in the LMCC's World Views program in 1999, sound artist Stephen Vitiello began recording sounds from his studio on the ninety-first floor of Tower One of the World Trade Center. Although he couldn't have predicted that the recordings would serve as a memorial, they can't help but be listened to as such, the uncanny reverberations of a place that no longer exists, a haunt haunted by haunting sonic resonances: creaking and rumbling that resembles phantoms moving furniture or sending messages crackling with static. Metal clanks gently, wind whistles low, and traffic floats up one thousand feet from street level. In his autobiography, Malcolm X writes of another space of reverence, the church: "It was spooky, with ghosts and spirituals and 'ha'nts' . . ." I know this only because the Oxford English Dictionary refers to this sentence in its definition of "haunt." Malcolm X was keenly aware of what Vitiello's recordings reveal about hallowed grounds, that they amass sentiments, they can predict disaster, and they hold histories that are sticky with the uncanny, a strangely familiar, restless home that is not home.

For the next twenty years, Lana often passed by the nearly 3,000 mailing labels placed on the tiled wall corridor between Fourteenth and Sixteenth Streets at Union Square Station, an Avery sticker for each person who died on September 11, 2001. It took John Lin and sixteen or so friends about two hours to put up this unassuming memorial, longer than it took for the Twin Towers to fall. The South Tower toppled to the ground fifty-seven minutes after it was hit, and fifty minutes later the North Tower succumbed to its fatal blow. People continue to commemorate those whom they grieve by taping down the peeling labels, adding personal notes to them or tracing over the letters that have worn away with time. Lana ordinarily rushes past this humble testament, but she feels a sense of muted pride that she shares a surname with this artist she does not know.

I was in my first semester of my first full-time teaching job when I heard about the attack. When sustaining prolonged visits between Canada and the U.S. became untenable, I had taken a one-year position as a visiting professor at Middle Tennessee

State University. It was a Tuesday, so I was teaching the Foundations Sculpture 3D class. I was probably giving out assignments when the art history professor pulled me aside and said that something was happening that I might want to see. But we were in the art building which was a converted barn lacking anything as fancy as a TV, so we listened to the radio that the receptionist had turned on. I went to my office, fortunately next to the classroom, and tried to call Lana.

I couldn't reach her, so I called her sister who was subletting a loft in Chinatown. Unlike Lana, Cynthia did have a cell phone and picked up while she was on a bus in Queens. I asked how she was doing and she started to cry. She had been on her way to Houston when the driver turned back, realizing that the airport was shutting down. Pedestrians were lugging suitcases down the road with no public transportation, taxis, or rental cars taking passengers.

On September 15, Lana was scheduled to visit me. Her calendar from that day reads: "All day attempt to fly to Nashville —Metropolitan Museum, reading, and address input, as well as some strange meetings with United Nations worker and art gallery buyer." Further context has vanished from her memory. Had she not jotted down these notes she would not be able to retrieve even this bare minimum of facts.

Once she managed to leave New York, Lana would end up staying in Tennessee for close to two weeks since all classes in the City University system were canceled for three weeks.

More often than not, it was I who traveled to New York. Every departure from my newfound home with Lana to my unfamiliar temporary residence in Murfreesboro was unsettling. This disjuncture reached an extreme upon my return from my first trip post 9/11. I opened the door and was hit with a stench that almost made me sick. On the phone that night I told Lana that I must have forgotten to flush the toilet. It wasn't until twenty years later that the incident came up again. We were driving down a twisting road late at night when I began to narrate to Lana a cautionary tale my elders told to scare me and my sisters into habitually flushing the toilet.

Ma lai rút ruột is a nocturnal female spirit in Vietnamese folklore. She is often pictured as a suspended head with her entrails dangling from her neck. This demon has one purpose: to eat your shit. She is known as Krasue in Thailand, Ahp in Cambodia, Penanggal in Malaysia, and Manananggal in the Phillippines. During daylight hours, ma lai rút ruột perambulates among the living, dissembling as a young, beauteous woman; at night, she disassembles, detaching from her lower core, rising above the earth only to descend upon putrid matter. The lore warns that those whose excrement is eaten by the fiend are destined to suffer from inextinguishable hunger, a ceaseless starvation regardless of the quantities they consume. Like vampires, ma lai rút ruột must reunite with her body before dawn breaks or be scorched by sunlight and reduced to ash.

Given the ghost stories I was reared upon, I am almost certain that if I'd gone number two before leaving for NYC, I would have flushed the toilet for fear of ma lai rút ruột. Also, not to be too graphic, but the load I found when I got home was larger than I would be accustomed to emitting. Tennessee is a red state, and Murfreesboro aligns with the state's political stance. As a butch Vietnamese, I never felt welcome. The young straight couple next door used to eye me as I came in late after work. At first, I would greet them, but when they never responded, I dropped the formality and words never passed between us. Usually, it is Lana who is tight-lipped with strangers, instructing me on how to erect an impenetrable barrier that will deter overly curious Uber drivers, gabbing airline companions, even the hapless tourist with a dead phone. I never revealed this to Lana until we were driving down that winding road, but I always had the discomforting suspicion that that couple was somehow connected with the bomb that was dropped in my bathroom, a vile gift meant to tempt evil spirits, leaving me with filthy remains to expunge.

Lana seldom records news and world events in her journals and calendars, but on September 11, 2001 she wrote, "WTC & Pentagon attacked," and on October 7, 2001, "U.S. bombs Afghanistan." Lana never felt herself a part of the narrative of the U.S. as a nation, but she did and does feel herself a part of the life of New York City. She felt that Union Square belonged to her as much as it belonged to anyone, because she went there almost every day for over a decade. John Lin's unsanctioned action on September 10, 2002, reaffirmed to Lana that Union Square subway station was "her" station.

On December 18, 2021, Lana and I signed the papers to become domestic partners and celebrated by purchasing two-for-one pairs of Fleuvog shoes that neither of us wore often because they fit poorly despite their fabulous style. The following year we moved up to Washington Heights. At that point, Lana claimed ownership over another subway station: 181st Street, a stop she had scarcely heard of after fourteen years of living in NYC, a station that signified a radically different relationship to the metropolis. Her friends would ask when she was coming to the city, and she would impatiently reply, "I'm *in* the city."

They would say, "Well, I mean, downtown."

•

When we moved to Washington Heights, we were pleased that it would be a quick subway ride to City College in Harlem. But after only one semester of this prized commute, upon being approved for tenure, Lana quit her job and took her first extended trip to Asia with a Fulbright Foundation Creative & Performing Arts Grant. For many, the tenure track leads to Shangri-La, but for Lana it felt like being trapped on the Snowpiercer, perpetually circling a frozen planet with an oppressively hierarchical coterie. On the crest of our honeymoon phase, the prospect of a year abroad tantalized us. We flew to Taiwan at the beginning of November 2003.

In March 2003 the World Health Organization had issued a global alert about an unknown pneumonia in Việt Nam and Hong Kong. On March 15, the WHO heightened the alert and issued emergency guidance to those traveling to Singapore and Canada. By April, Severe Acute Respiratory Syndrome (SARS) was identified as an infectious disease caused by a novel coronavirus. But by July, Taiwan had been removed from the list of areas affected by SARS, signifying the official end of the outbreak. Avian flu had also been reported in Asia, which led us to curtail our eating choices but didn't deter our travel. We were reassured by and even grew impatient with the vigilance of safety measures we encountered, such as automatic temperature screening at airports via infrared cameras. Our relative youth and absolute inexperience with epidemics made us fearless in this regard. We did not perceive ourselves as risk-takers. Lana had already taken what could be seen as a life-altering risk, jumping off the tenure train, and I had already taken the risk of joining Lana in NYC without a long-term job or working papers.

Our ten months in Taiwan kicked off with three frantic days scrambling to find an apartment. After seeing two apartments on top floors, one of which was scarcely more than a squalid shell, we were disabused of our presumption that the rooftop apartment is a coveted spot, as it is in Western urban centers. As the most vulnerable targets of inclement weather, rooftop apartments were variously too hot, too cold, too damp, and too windy for local residents and were inevitably rented to foreigners. From our roof you could glimpse mountains between the water-stained concrete buildings and our neighbor slapping himself at pressure points, accompanied by an electronic melody issuing from a truck or a power tool of some sort somewhere below.

In Taiwan it was not uncommon for people of all ages, sizes, and social classes to exercise in public, whether it was a doorman flexing his limbs or a group of elders practicing tai chi in the park. Once, we caught two women teaching each other dance moves in a hotel lobby. Another night we chanced upon people ballroom dancing in a basketball court wearing athletic shoes, clunky, inelegant footwear so elegantly coordinated to complex moves. This serendipitous encounter might have been the source of inspiration for our brief foray into gay dance lessons from a place called Stepping Out when we returned to New York. It was an exercise in humility since we both wanted to lead, or, rather, Lana was willing to follow, but I was unable to lead. One evening we were not paired together. My partner was a short, feisty woman, even smaller than Lana. I praised her authoritative, guiding embrace while Lana fumed.

On the roof in Taipei we would attempt to dry our laundry, but since it was perpetually humid, any absorbent material carried a latent dampness. Lana loathes even a hint of mildew. When I was searching for a sublet for Lana to spend our first summer together in Toronto, I had asked her if there was anything in particular that she would prefer in terms of housing. She promptly replied that the single thing that revolted her was the smell of mildew. We expended a fair amount of energy during our time in Asia attempting to prevent the growth of mildew.

Our other primary activity was to produce a video. Lana had secured her Fulbright award for a solo project, but after prolonged conversations about the colonial legacy in Asia, we embarked on what would become our first completed collaboration. We recorded hours and hours of footage, the bulk of which we never used and which has been contained on tapes that only this past year were digitized so as to be available for review after nineteen years of storage. As Lana scans through it now, she ponders whether this is where all her memories went, locked into these fragile miniature cassettes, inaccessible within obsolete technology, silently degrading as the decades passed.

In the footage, Lana occasionally pans over and I see an image of myself. Someone has taken me aside to talk with me, often in a language I do not know. They gesture emphatically, and I nod with understanding. Like my mother who was able to communicate with her Chinese tenant despite lacking a shared maternal tongue, I am sometimes able to comprehend languages not my own, though not with her skill. In the U.S., Canada, everywhere I have traveled in the world, strangers will not infrequently cross the street or stop their cars to ask me for directions. Standing in front of a vertical mirror, a woman buttoning a pair of slacks will inquire how they look as I wait for Lana who is dressing behind the drawn curtains. Even something as intimate as a swimsuit will prompt a changing room companion to ask for my opinion. Lana suspects that I emit some kind of signal or vibration that those in need instinctively pick up on. Kindness emanates from you, she postulates, as if it were a rare scent that is only perceptible when sought after.

Deprived since childhood of the street food I cherished, I was overjoyed with the gustatory variety of Taiwanese night markets. More than an opportunity for outdoor dining, these were an overload for the senses: deafening, relentless shouting, recorded advertisements blaring over megaphones, revving motorcycles, traditional stringed instruments, honking horns, unmuffled motors, buzzing insects sizzling in electric blue light traps. The auditory stimuli competed with olfactory sensations of stinky tofu, aromatic durian, flowery incense, pungent teas, and persistent mildew embedded in clothing, towels, and dish rags. The visual feast of shiny plastic goods, glowing lanterns, waving flags, glaring cellophane-wrapped snacks, and bodies and bodies and bodies pushing, shoving, and bustling, whirred in my brain as I thought, echoing a phrase from a movie I hadn't seen: I see Asians. It had been many years, decades even, since I had been crowded by Asians, where I might get lost in a mass of people who looked like me.

While in Taipei, we witnessed firsthand the opening of Taipei 101, Taiwan's version of the World Trade Center. We watched an interminable stream of people riding up and down the escalators, and then filing one after the other around the maze of glistening corridors, reminiscent of an army of ants. The Taipei metro is likewise modern, precise, clean, a source of civic pride. The automated voice that gently reminds riders of each stop repeats the station names in four different languages: Mandarin, Taiwanese, Hakka, and English. Riding the MRT brown line from Zhongshan Jr. High School, the station nearest to our apartment, to the southernmost station, Taipei Zoo, at the end of the line, I could see why Taiwan was named Formosa, beautiful island, by the Portuguese—the countryside is verdant with acacias, lianas, banyans, figs, banana trees.

We also enrolled in a Chinese language class together. I compare our two notebooks side by side: Lana begins with

"I'm wrong; my mistake," followed by "I only speak English"; I begin with "I'm almost ready." My notebook contains Vietnamese diacritics that were meant to aid me in pronunciation and tone, but my Vietnamese accent always gave me away as a foreigner, an outsider on a lower rung of the social ladder. After nine months of Chinese lessons, the length of time it takes to gestate a human being, I proudly ordered my favorite shaved-ice dessert and received a plate of bananas, the only fruit I dislike. But getting a food order wrong was only an inconvenience compared to the sharp disappointment of experiencing how my speech betrayed my status. Many Asians are guilty of an internalized racism that elevates whiteness and denigrates fellow Asians who are considered of lower class.

Most Vietnamese in Taiwan are what would be called undocumented migrant workers in the U.S. If they are female, they came as caregivers, house cleaners, "wives," or, in fact, all three at once. I was perplexing to most Taiwanese and Vietnamese we encountered because I could not be clearly categorized as any of the above. My hair was buzz cut, which I would justify to inquirers as a solution to the extreme heat. I didn't have regular employment and I wasn't allied to an institution. The precarity of being a foreigner has persisted throughout Lana's and my life together. It was not unique to Asia. It has punctuated our shared existence, though in Asia we would come to feel our sacrifices acutely. They cut into the flesh of our relatively tender relationship. But we made a choice to remain with each other. We managed to suture the wounds, and, like a scar, a different kind of strength has emerged where once was a fragile fissure.

Lana always felt a foreigner to "family." In Taiwan she was continually on the verge of understanding the words coming out of strangers' mouths, strangers who sounded to her like relatives, because she'd only heard family members speak Taiwanese in the U.S. It was a language she could not speak but to which she bore an intimate relation. No doubt she'd heard through the walls of her mother's womb and later the walls of her bedroom as her parents spoke in Taiwanese, the words they shouted into that black rotary phone that hung from the wall. She could understand bits and pieces but could never grasp the narrative as a whole.

If you learn even a few words of Chinese your ears will quickly tune into the phrase *mei guanxi*, which you will hear on a daily basis. *Guanxi* refers to the maintenance of the network of good social relations. As far as I could tell, one rarely speaks of *guanxi*—it is the invisible ground upon which all human interactions rest. But the negative of *guanxi*, *mei guanxi*, is constantly invoked. Translated literally as "no relation," it has the meaning of "it doesn't matter" and is used to alleviate embarrassment resulting from some kind of faux pas. But as much as someone might try to assure you that something is of no matter, is not important, has no relation or relevance, *guanxi* lurks below. *Mianzi*, the concept of "face," denotes one's social position, status, and prestige within this network of relations. I am familiar with the Vietnamese variation of "face," having been indoctrinated in it since I was a child. I recognize in my interactions with most Southeast and East Asians a delicate dynamic of "saving face" or "losing face."

When Lana visited Taiwan, her family, who are inculcated in *guanxi*, went wildly out of their way to be good hosts, taking her to see temples and train stations to help with the films that she was engrossed in making. Lana used the camera as a defensive device to protect her from the disorientation that crushed her spirit in this land of kin that was neither birthplace nor adopted home. A camera thrust up between herself and the world would act as shield, a two-way mirror through which she could spy on others and pretend that they could not see and therefore not harm her. It was her portable window, the way she liked to think of windows. For the most part, my presence helped. I took the place of the camera; I was a human prosthetic that mediated external dangers for Lana. But we also had our most dramatic fights about "face" because Lana wanted to refuse it; she wanted *mei guanxi* to really mean *mei guanxi*. I knew that to exist in Asia meant that relations always mattered.

Traveling in a foreign country in the early to mid 2000s was more challenging than it is now. We couldn't rely on GPS, Google

Translate, Airbnb, or Uber. Lana carried around a creased scrap of paper with her dad's ballpoint pen characters for "where to catch bus," "where to buy ticket," "which platform?" We asked our Chinese language teacher to write "which side view better," "sit in front seat." I would be the one to vocalize, whether to ask questions, order food, or give directions, even though I possessed only a smattering of Chinese whereas Lana had taken beginner's Chinese off and on for years as a young adult. I was more capable of speaking Chinese because I wasn't afraid to sound like an idiot. I wasn't mortified of failure as Lana was. I dove in with the same fervor I had when I plunged into English, because I understood, as with swimming, that mastering the new can only be accomplished by abandoning inhibition. Lana remains a poor swimmer despite repeated lessons that found her clinging to the side of the pool or sinking when directed to float. I was well acquainted with the dictate that respect was gained through proper speech. I trained myself on the correct English pronunciation of "thirteen," and I drilled my mother and little sister on the same. "They will always mistreat you if you cannot speak well," I would intone. When Lana and I were seeking a woman who could speak Shanghainese for our film project, I culled together the few words I knew: "*Wo yao nu ren.* (I want a woman.)" I learned from an early age that sometimes only speech can save you.

We couldn't spend almost a year abroad without returning to my homeland, and Lana had yet to visit Việt Nam. We landed at Tân Sơn Nhất International Airport on February 10, 2004, twenty-four years since I had last been in Việt Nam. The world shrank in that quarter of a century. It is Asian tradition that someone who has departed their homeland must honor their forebears immediately upon returning. Lana was familiar with this ritual from her grandmother's funeral, though as a non-Taiwanese Taiwanese she does not follow the filial law to the letter. I however was immediately to head from the airport to my grandmother's village of Bến Tre, an exhausting journey during which we needed to stop by a streetside shack to request the use of a toilet for Lana who could no longer contain her bursting bladder. Lana silently climbed back into the car. She did not speak about her horror at the creatures that clamored around the drain and spilled onto the floor, a black, vibrating mass that made her skin crawl. Living in NYC had taught Lana that cockroaches will likely outlast humans by millennia, but she was still a suburbanite at her core, having only been bothered throughout her childhood by an occasional moth or cricket.

We stayed in Bến Tre only long enough for me to realize that what I remembered as my grandmother's palatial estate was a modest, even slightly cramped, abode. On the day we departed, we rose at dawn when the moon was still a sliver of a thumbnail. Roosters crowed as we hurriedly piled ourselves onto the back of my uncle's scooter, me grabbing him and Lana grabbing me as he sped to the ferry to take us to our next destination, Vũng Tàu, where my aunt lived and where my family used to vacation. Here Lana sulked as I ignored Valentine's Day. It was easy for me to convince Lana not to buy into holidays created for commercial purposes, but she enjoyed romance, so we tried to inject it into our trip, fairly unsuccessfully. In Hội An, for example, what we hoped would be a romantic sunset tour of the Thu Bồn River turned into an opportunity for the fisherwoman rowing the sampan boat to unravel her entire life story. To maintain *guanxi* I would give her a generous tip whether or not I enjoyed the trip.

Later, in Hà Nội, Lana suffered from food poisoning after eating noodles at the Đà Nẵng Airport. Exhaustion caused us to drop our guard; we may even have ordered eel. After she recovered, we set off to Long Biên Bridge to do some recording. When we viewed the footage back in our hotel room, Lana was especially impressed with the quantity, scale, and range of objects that people, most frequently older women, ported on their bicycles. The audio, however, was unusable because of the distracting assaults of wind. Someone at the hotel told us about a former TV guy who might be able to help. We commissioned him to make a microphone wind shield since no one could tell us where one might be purchased.

He devised what was essentially a sock. Lana was appalled. She brooded as I thanked him graciously. There was no discussion about payment in his presence because of "face," and we were both put on scooters to take us back to our hotel. The young man driving me was the TV guy's nephew or cousin, and he pulled over at a street market on the side of the road where I was to buy an expensive bottle of liquor for his uncle—not Black Label, because Vietnamese aren't fond of it, but maybe some sort of cognac. It was when I returned to the hotel that Lana and I had our most explosive argument to date. We were on an extremely tight budget, living as two on a stipend for one. To Lana, a sock masquerading as a windshield had no right to command the price of a bottle of liquor. She could have bought a sock or maybe even a dozen at the market for a couple of U.S. dollars. It infuriated her that asking the TV guy to re-fashion the sock or come up with something better would require yet another potentially more substantial gift. Our impassioned dispute probably extinguished itself through enervation and resignation. Ironically, the sock proved priceless. In the succeeding two decades, what has become known between us as "the sock incident" never fails to amuse us.

We faced more hardship in that year abroad than our immature relationship had yet endured, but we always returned to each other. Tempestuous battles concluded with us walking away from each other only to find one another at the same bookstore, or, even more unexpectedly, at a niche library to which neither of us had ever previously ventured. I don't know if I would have admitted that I felt lost without Lana, but I know that when we met, we were both found. As Lana would later glean from Freud's *Three Essays on the Theory of Sexuality*, the finding of our first sexual object is a re-finding of it. We find ourselves in each other, and we keep re-finding ourselves with each other. Before Lana, I anticipated aging alone. But I also sent a message into the universe with my three criteria for a life partner: someone with whom I could laugh, discuss art and ideas, and dance—yes, and dance. Though our dancing leaves something to be desired, we dance beside each other, neither one leading nor following.

During a mid-year Fulbright check-in, Lana and I learned about former Vietnamese refugee camps that had been turned into driving ranges and family recreation centers, and we trekked to the outskirts of Hong Kong to document them. After close to a year in Asia, this last project, to which we devoted several weeks, was the most gratifying, although it never felt complete. So, about six years later, in 2010, when we had an invitation to exhibit work in Hong Kong, we decided to extend the project and visit my own former refugee camp at Pulau Bidong, Malaysia. I winced at the idea of telling a sob story, tearfully rehearsing my memories as I roamed the site of my childhood confinement with a shaky handheld camera. Cue sentimental music to swell during the sound mix. But Lana assured me that we would never embark on such a project, and she located an all-inclusive resort in Merang, Terrenganu, Malaysia.

To call it a resort makes it sound much fancier than it was—their website uses the term "rustic"—but it had the distinction of being positioned directly across from Bidong Island, with not much more than eight nautical miles of the South China Sea between. The view from Sutra Beach Resort struck me as surreal. Here I was granted a vantage point upon a place that had been crucial to my survival; it was a perspective I had not been privileged to have until that moment, thirty years after my escape from Việt Nam. When I'd departed my childhood home with only some of my immediate family members, wearing the hand-me-down clothing that would serve as the only remnants of my former life, I could not foresee my future arrival on Bidong. For all I knew I might not emerge from the journey alive. Below the deck of a fishing boat, I could not see our approach to the island. Nor would I have the opportunity to view it when we left a number of months later, destined for Canada. I spent many tedious afternoons on the shores of Bidong, missing my mom and little sister who stayed behind in Sài Gòn, and my eldest sister, Trang, who was in a camp in Singapore. If my adolescent thoughts wandered toward the future, my mind's eye never envisioned me standing upon the mainland gazing at a horizon that held both my present and past. As a forty-two-year-old adult at Sutra Beach Resort I stared at a postcard version of my youth; could I perceive a trace of the twelve-year-old tomboy I had been?

Lana and I did not sign up for a group tour with former refugees or purchase a scuba diving package, partially because of the expense, partially because of timing, and mostly because we wanted to spend our time as we wished. A hotel staff person hooked us up with a couple of local fishermen. We met them early in the morning, carrying with us a modest semiprofessional digital camera, a snapshot camera, a lightweight tripod, a portable digital video camera, and Burt's Bees mosquito repellent. We wore baseball caps and linen long sleeve shirts, but we were gravely ill-prepared for a jungle hike.

We did not dock at the jetty that day. The fishermen let the tide carry the boat up to shore and we scrambled out. As we took a right, my eye glanced upon a beaten-up vessel cast on the sand like a beached metallic whale. We uncovered a porcelain squat toilet overgrown with grass and a tin canister with a yellow label not too far away. And then we decided to make our way into the jungle. Our photo documentation gives the impression of a deserted area that time forgot. Photographs can lend a sense of placid calm to a site or situation that is anything but. I took a lot of blurry pictures, some with streaks that suggest the harried quality of our expedition. Mosquitoes swarmed us and we were bathed in sweat that made it challenging to focus physically and mentally or even to keep our eyeglasses clear. We stumbled onto what I guessed were large water tanks, covered with moss and roots crawling along their surface like veins. A pipe faced the structure where another pipe protruded, their open mouths perhaps meant to be fitted together. A tree branch grew out of the pipe's interior like an alien bifurcated tongue. We photographed rusted metal structures that had completely collapsed, entangled with branches and strewn with leaves, and a television with a cracked screen. Fighting our way through the patch of jungle to a clearing, we came upon a house with all its vertical beams and corrugated metal remaining, but none of its walls intact, so we could see clear through to the trees surrounding it. This photograph gives an impression of its taking; it is slightly overexposed and thus hints at the blinding sunlight that was overpowering us.

That evening we decided we had come too far not to spend more time on the island that surfaced from the water just beyond our window. A few days later the fishermen brought us back to Bidong, planning to return at the end of the day. This time we walked straight ahead and, after climbing a series of steep stone steps, stopped before a ramshackle pyramid of plaques memorializing the suffering of the dead. I never visited the temple when I was living in the camp, but I knew it was up what some called "Religion Hill." A headless Buddha stared off toward the South China Sea. A forest of incense sticks rose up from a pile of ashes at the base of a statue whose head was reduced to a core of metal wound around a concrete base. This solemn figure was flanked by two dragons with gaping mouths, metal exposed where parts of their noses and jaws were broken away. Lana had read about the Christian church that we came across later whose blue-tiled back wall still stood with a painted white cross in front of it.

Our photos document a blue plastic watering pitcher; seven overturned amber glass bottles buried purposefully in a bed of dried leaves, but to what end I do not know; two mismatched slippers; a bamboo pole with numbers painted on it in red, perhaps the shack or boat number. I don't recall being assigned a number during my time on the island nor do I remember a boat number, but I have seen former refugees identify themselves this way on blogs.

Lana recorded audio, listening to the waves sloshing at the jetty, the whining insects, the insistent birds. I was scavenging for our art project: cigarette wrappers and butts, pieces of tin foil, shards of pottery, seashells, oddly shaped coral. When I looked up Lana was standing in the water, her zip-off pant legs removed, her arms outstretched, holding her video camera facedown at the churning sea.

I was stashing flat powdery seashells like the ones I'd played with as a child into my messenger bag, when I received a text from the fishermen who were trying to find us. I called to Lana who was deep in her womb of video recording, mesmerized by the glints of light that wriggled and danced on the foamy crests. "We have to go!" I shouted. Perhaps she was groggy from too much sun because she blinked at me confused. "Get your things; we need to go, now."

"Isn't it early?" she complained as she padded to shore and grabbed her backpack.

"The weather is bad, so they want to take us back."

The fishermen materialized out of nowhere; we struggled aboard the boat and retreated from the island.

The vessel was tipping precariously on the tumultuous waves. I was aware of Lana's fear of the ocean and directed her to move to her side of the boat and grab its edge. If we capsized, I didn't know if I could save her. I wanted her to hold onto something more solid than me, but she refused. "If we're going down, we're going down together," she hissed into my ear, and so I hung on to her.

One of the fishermen was speaking into his cell phone. We didn't know if this meant he was unconcerned and chatting with a friend or whether he was calling the equivalent of the Southeast Asian coast guard. "I have two stupid tourists aboard and I don't want them dying on me," I imagined him saying. It hadn't occurred to me until that moment that I didn't know if there was a Malaysian coast guard. All I could think was how fucking mad I would be if I drowned in the very sea that I'd managed to survive three decades earlier, all for the sake of an art project.

Forty-five minutes later we'd reached the mainland without incident, in fact with less of a soaking than we'd once gotten on a ferry ride in the Long Island Sound, where wealthy residents get door-to-door service to their multimillion-dollar island "cottages." One of the fishermen sprang onto shore, and when we thanked them and asked how much we owed them, motioning the way one does when one wants a receipt at a restaurant, the man grabbed a stick and scratched a number in the sand. We paid him, he jumped up on his boat, and they sailed away, rushing to beat the weather. Lana and I looked at each other and then at the beach and laughed. "Well, I guess this is our receipt," we exclaimed.

The next morning, we would be leaving the resort. I carefully packed my artifacts in my luggage. Later I would give each of my sisters a seashell as a keepsake, and a few of them would find a home on the landing of my parents' staircase in Mississauga. Before we boarded the ferry, I caught sight of a modest pile of indigo globes nestled in a street vendor's cart. I stopped short and pointed at them. When given the price I did a quick calculation and handed the woman my remaining ringgit, announcing that I would take them all. Lana was aghast. "Do we need *all* of them?" she gasped as she tried to keep up while I hurried toward the dock, the laden plastic bag wagging in

unison with my stride. Once safely aboard, I tucked my trea-
sures into my backpack, abiding warnings I had heard from
relatives that some hotels forbid the portage of mangosteen on
the property because its wine-colored juice stains linens and
towels like blood. When we settled into our accommodations
in Kuala Terrenganu, we found a spot to sit outside on the
grounds. I reached in my pack and selected a perfect sphere,
which I cupped in the palms of my hands, a gesture of reverence, then I pressed against the resistant but pliable shell until
it cracked open to expose the tender white crescents huddled
together like peeled garlic cloves. I instructed Lana to suck out
the flesh, which she did. She rhapsodized about the exquisite
fusion of sweet and tart, a flavor it had been at least a quarter
of a century since I had savored. After consuming our entire
stash, we were left with bloodied fingers, ecstatic yet still craving more. We mournfully tossed out the shells, but not before
licking the interiors so as not to waste a drop of the precious
liquid.

•

When we returned from our Hong Kong/Malaysia trip in July
2010, Lana was to start her second year in a doctoral program
at NYU's Department of Media, Culture, and Communication,
which entitled her to health insurance after at least five years

uninsured. At the end of September, she had an appointment for a breast and transvaginal ultrasound. Until a nurse practitioner convinced her to get one, she didn't even know what a breast ultrasound was or that it might be an option in lieu of a mammogram. Lana had refused a mammogram because a woman in our building alarmed us with her horror story of a mammography machine breaking her rib. But when Lana arrived at the radiologist's office, they insisted on her getting a mammogram. She showed them her calendar appointment for a breast ultrasound. A mammogram appeared nowhere on her schedule. She tried to resist but they mechanically ordered her to take off her shirt, pushed her toward the machine, positioned her arm, and Lana mechanically complied. She was still seething about not being heard when the upper and lower portions of the machine squeezed together and produced blood on the plate. In the instant of seeing the droplets, Lana connected them to the blood stains that had appeared on a T-shirt she wore to bed several months before, which she had ignored. An expression of sympathy mixed with a tacit "I told you so" flitted across the nurse's face as she gruffly cleaned off the plate, almost scolding her patient for contaminating it.

After her first biopsy, Lana went to Bobst Library and read a book about CT scans for a seminar on the cultures of biomedicine in which she was coincidentally enrolled. It was difficult to concentrate. Foreboding thoughts kept invading the lines on the page, but Lana kept swatting them away as annoyances. No one had made a definitive pronouncement. All of this was precautionary. But there was blood on the plate. This might be slightly more than routine, but nothing was certain. I didn't go with Lana to the first biopsy because the word "cancer" had been studiously avoided. I did, however, accompany Lana to her second biopsy and to almost every other appointment for the next year and beyond. It would be years before Lana could convince me that it wasn't necessary to accompany her to all medical appointments.

The radiologist used the metaphor of grapes. Invasive ductal carcinoma branches out like a cluster of grapes. This seemed a particularly cruel analogy as grapes are one of my favorite fruits. After the doctor's mini lecture, he asked what we would like to do. Lana asked if it was possible to do nothing. He could not contain his look of horror and responded firmly, "No, this is cancer. You can't do nothing."

When Lana was getting dressed, I was standing alone in the waiting room. It was eerily quiet in the Upper East Side clinic. This was before we became something less than a cog in the Memorial Sloan Kettering machine; just a number, Lana's birthdate, repeated ad nauseum at every single encounter. There were no other patients paging through magazines, no television blaring. The street traffic seemed to have been put on pause and there wasn't a pedestrian in sight. If it had been Lana in the waiting room, she would have thought it was like a scene from *The Last Man on Earth* or the *Twilight Zone* episode "Time Enough at Last," the one where Burgess Meredith survives a nuclear holocaust that destroys everyone and everything on Earth except the books in the public library. Lana might wonder if there were any correlations between her own predicament and Henry Bemis's; Burgess Meredith's character hates people and loves books but has broken his only means of accessing them, his thick spectacles. I don't have those kind of movie and TV references. Instead, I pondered how much time we would have together, whether I might lose my person who had finally found me, and how I could shape up to be the person she needed.

The radiologist made us an appointment with his favored surgeon. We went to it and found her to be chilly. She was very matter of fact. This was garden-variety breast cancer. She would just lop it off, and maybe take off the other one for good measure. According to cancer standards, at forty-four, Lana was still rather young, so more aggressive treatment now would pay off in later years. Lana was not particularly attached to her breasts, but she was attached to research. Her seminar on biomedicine scrutinized the medical-industrial complex. She resisted the unquestioning performance of the compliant patient. Contrary to her parents' advice, she couldn't simply do what the doctor told her. Even if she were to attempt to follow such advice, she believed it was inherently flawed. There wasn't to be a single doctor and "he" wasn't going to tell her what to do.

The next medical procedures were an fMRI and an MRI-guided core biopsy. Because the initial biopsies and fMRI had been relatively pain free, Lana was not overly anxious about the MRI-guided biopsy. We sat together in the waiting area, Lana enveloped in an oversized robe, clenching her fist up at her neck where she held together the two sides that were not designed to close around a small frame. She perpetually shivered in the temperature-controlled medical environments and was not yet practiced in bringing a hat and scarf. Often, I would still need to give her my jacket or sweater, which I would drape around her shoulders over the ill-fitting robes. A young man, probably an intern, bustled in and rushed through a series of disclosures. I could scarcely keep up with him but suddenly the procedure sounded terrifying. Lana took on the sullen demeanor of the Angry Little Asian Girl as she does when she opposes something that she feels disempowered to reject. When the voice concluded on a question that sounded like a statement, Lana murmured, "Not that I can think of." The man promptly disappeared with clipboard in hand, and Lana and I stared at each other. She waited a moment and then whispered, "Do you think we can make a run for it?"

Once it was decided that doing nothing was not an option, a mastectomy was the easiest choice. Lana selected an Italian surgeon from Memorial Sloan Kettering for his impeccable reputation and tailored suits, and I couldn't disagree. I was petrified of the surgery and told Lana that she should invite lots of friends to the hospital or they might not treat her as well. "As well as what?" she queried. "You mean they will give someone better treatment if they're popular?"

"They'll just know that people care for you . . ." I submitted.

"And if anything goes wrong, your friends might sue for malpractice," she concluded.

In retrospect, I think I wanted a support team more for myself than for her. She was, after all, asleep for most of it, while I had to wait, and wait, and wait. Matthew and a couple of other close friends waited with me, including Kristine, who altered the mastectomy bra they supplied because it was too large for Lana. The bespoke bra was stitched with Lana's nickname and a heart floating where her breast would have been. Lana would re-use it when she had to undergo a "completion" mastectomy a year later because the margins of her nipple-sparing mastectomy were not clear of cancer. She now regrets not having the other nipple removed because it is only annoying to her at this point, but she doesn't feel like an annoying nipple warrants another surgery. I sympathize with her wish to be spared an unwanted appendage and would welcome the opportunity to have my own breasts, those outward female attributes, removed for free.

After the surgery, her Italian surgeon referred Lana to a renowned Italian radiologist with whom we fantasized he was having an affair. The radiation oncologist said it was a shame because she would have recommended a lumpectomy with radiation. But Lana had no qualms about the mastectomy. A lumpectomy for her breast size would practically equate to a mastectomy given that the core biopsies were almost sufficient to make her flat. The deployment of an invisible lethal agent threatened her more than the skillful wielding of a knife. The blade is a favored tool for woodworking and culinary arts, spheres of activity that are figuratively close to her heart, perhaps because of my fondness for them. When I expressed concern about the dangers of targeting radiation on someone as diminutive as Lana, one of the three medical students milling around in the claustrophobic room brushed me off with, "We do our best to avoid the heart." Lana was unconvinced of the merits of radiation, though she did not begrudge the office visit for the thrill of ogling the doctor's impressive over-the-knee leather boots.

Because her tumor was estrogen receptive, another medical option Lana considered was an oophorectomy. She consulted a gynecologic oncologist about the potential benefits of removing her ovaries. "If estrogen feeds my breast cancer, and I don't want to have children, why would I want to keep my ovaries?" Lana beseeched.

The gynecologic oncologist replied, "I really can't advise you on breast cancer. It's not my organ." Lana returned his blank stare. She later found some evidence of a higher mortality rate for women who had undergone oophorectomy, although the studies did not align perfectly with her specific case.

Repeatedly Lana was disappointed in the medical estab-
lishment and wider culture's equation between womanhood
and body parts associated with women. It was as if losing one's
hair, breasts, or ovaries would be more concerning than living a
long childless life with one's intelligence intact. It was suggested
that one might actually prefer a less favorable survival rate for
the option of preserving enviable locks, symmetrical breasts,
or the ability to produce offspring. Partially spurred by Audre
Lorde's anecdote about a perky Reach For Recovery volunteer
who proudly asks Lorde to identify which of her breasts is real,
Lana also contacted the American Cancer Society's volunteer
program and was demoralized by the silence on the other end
of the call when Lana mentioned that breast cancer is not ex-
clusively a woman's disease. Most of the services and support
groups she availed herself of at the time were alienating.

Lana was preoccupied with the possibility of long-term
cognitive impairment and posed a question about chemo-brain
to a breast-cancer discussion group. When she was bemoaning
the lack of longitudinal studies about chemo-brain with Matthew, he volunteered that his partner at the time, Cara, had
spotted the same type of questions online.

"Really?" Lana said dubiously. "I never see anything about
this."

Matthew held the phone away from his mouth and asked
Cara about the post. He came back on the line and said Cara

would check to see if there were any responses. Lana broke into hysterical laughter when she recognized the username as her own.

When I heard this anecdote, I felt a measure of pride because Lana was posting under the name of her favorite piece of furniture. Before I entered her life, Lana would have taken little note of furniture. Not only did I once need to explain to her the difference between a couch and a sofa, I had to justify the need to acquire the latter. She thought of furniture, if she thought of it at all, as purely functional, and deliberated at length as to whether or not a piece of furniture was even necessary. Did we really *need* a sofa? Wouldn't two chairs do? Did we really *need* a bed; she had been doing fine with a futon. I had to convince her that a sofa was not only a surface upon which to sit, it could be an aesthetic object as well as a place of reflection. This was before Lana began psychoanalytic training, which naturally alerted her to the importance of "the couch," but created mild confusion at the distinction between a sofa and a couch by non-analytic standards. I reasoned that we could lie together upon a sofa whereas we would be segregated on chairs, and reminded her that she could lie with her head in my lap, which had become a beloved position for both of us. It was a position we often took during those chemo days, until the fast zooms and swish pans on the TV made her nauseous.

"What would you do?" Lana asked. She had a habit of asking for advice and then not taking it, which can be annoying.

"If you don't want my advice, why do you ask for it?" I protested.

"I want to hear what you have to say," she responded unsatisfactorily. Lana would scrupulously collect the advice of her confidantes, compare and contrast it, and then mull over decisions indefinitely. But there are some decisions that cannot be deferred and some things that cannot be definitively answered. This bothered Lana enormously. I told her that if I were diagnosed with cancer, I might not seek treatment, at least not allopathic treatment.

Lana retorted, "But why not, if it works?"

"I don't know, maybe because I wouldn't want to suffer. Maybe because it would be my time." I have Buddhist leanings and a stronger belief in fate than Lana does, who sometimes equates the acceptance of what one cannot change with resignation.

Irritated, Lana blurted out, "I wouldn't want you to die if you didn't have to."

"I want you to live, but I don't want you to suffer," I countered.

No one predicted Lana would die from this bout of cancer. The question really had to do with how to "change the natural history of your breast cancer," as her medical oncologist put it. "We don't know what to do with this is the honest answer," the doctor admitted. "In some ways you fall through the cracks in our present staging system." This acknowledgement of Lana's sense of ever-present uncertainty and lack of fit with her environment, which she had experienced well before her cancer diagnosis, was affirming, and affirmation is what Lana continually sought.

When Lana first started teaching full-time and was struck by the non-responsive bowed heads of her students, one of them, seeing her exasperation, ventured, "What, do you need constant affirmation?" Lana did not hesitate to mentally affirm that she does.

"You don't need to decide now. Do you want to think about it?" the doctor suggested.

"No. I'm tired of thinking about it," Lana confessed. "What would you do?"

"I would do ECT," her oncologist assured her. And so, Lana decided on dose-dense chemotherapy.

Initially Lana had selected a Vietnamese oncologist who proceeded as if her treatment plan was not a choice. "Likely you've had this for a few years," the doctor postulated. She resorted to a construction metaphor combined with the most common metaphor for cancer, the military metaphor. She talked about using surgery and chemotherapy to chip off bricks as well as to clear the dust in order to "win the battle."

I found the Vietnamese oncologist brutal. Lana agreed she was indelicate. After meeting with her twice, Lana was ready to switch oncologists, but was told that this wasn't allowed. And then, through scouring online breast cancer discussion groups, she was given the idea that the effective way of changing doctors was not to explain one's preferences but to put the onus on scheduling. Lana called MSKCC and reported that she was only able to have her chemotherapy infusions on Thursdays, coinciding with the day the desired oncologist worked and that the original oncologist did not work. She felt vindicated when she later discovered that her chosen doctor had been the oncologist of Eve Kosofsky Sedgwick, to whom Lana had, by this point, devoted a chapter of her dissertation.

Cancer was a full-time job for both of us. After the battery of tests and appointments, the agony of decision making, the frustrating holes of research and contradiction, Lana withstood treatment, and I helped sustain her. I wrote email updates to her family and learned how to cook nourishing, healthful food. We embarked on a year of organic, gluten-free, low salt, clean living. I would brew giant tureens of broth from scratch, slowly simmering leeks, celery, sweet potatoes, mushrooms, and onions to leech out their cancer-fighting properties. I would make ice cubes of freshly squeezed juice for Lana to suck on during chemotherapy, because I heard that ice chips could reduce mouth sores.

Lana would go running and lavish praise upon steroids. When her treatment was over, she would sometimes reminisce about how steroids allowed her to climb the hills at Fort Tryon

Park. She was also somewhat nostalgic about the supple texture and gentle curl of her hair post-chemo. Aside from steroids and six months to a year of good hair, there was one other positive aspect of chemo, which was the cessation of her menstrual period. She was not officially post-menopausal; it was apparently termed "chemical menopause." But in any case, Lana was very pleased to be rid of her period, and I cannot say that I did not envy her a little. I, too, would have been relieved not to bear the "woman's curse."

During her eleven weeks of epirubicin, cyclophosphamide, and paclitaxel chemotherapy, Lana would retire early and lie in bed, her ears filled with her thunderous pulse. "At least I know I'm alive," she meditated, partly distressed and partly stunned by the sensation of her blood coursing through her chest and limbs and collecting at her temples. I stayed up watching *Chopped* and *Iron Chef*, worried that if I fell asleep, I wouldn't wake if Lana needed me. For all of Lana's equivocations and anxieties, she was not as fearful as I. She was determined, and, as always, analytical.

As I grew more confident that no crisis would transpire if I left home, I tried to take advantage of cancer support systems myself. I attended the caregiver support group at the LGBTQ Center downtown. I would spend two hours on the train, an hour at the session, and come home more emotionally drained each time. It was a group of six and every story was worse than the next. I felt guilty, but I didn't have the capacity to take on another person's burdens while caring for my own person. After three devastating sessions, I switched to individual visits with a Latinx social worker who was very easy to talk to.

I would get off the subway at Twenty-fifth Street and go to Whole Foods. Even though I always left the house caffeinated, I would order the super sweet matcha and an almond croissant covered with powdered sugar. These were my only rebellions against the otherwise strictly healthful diet I kept with Lana. I had the urge to fuel myself for therapy, whereas with an earlier therapist Lana had connected me to through her psychoanalytic training institute, I felt the need to replenish myself after each session. I would shut my first therapist's office door and walk straight to Beacon's Closet and buy myself a tie. I got three ties out of that experience; one of them is Dolce Gabbana. By my calculation this could have meant forty-four or forty-eight ties for the year, depending upon the therapist's summer break. Lana was eager for me to talk to the analyst-in-training about why I was compelled to purchase a tie after every meeting. But since I owned close to fifty ties already, I opted to terminate without processing my impulses.

I received a finite number of free sessions with the second therapist through CancerCare, and when I went through them all, I brought my gratis therapist potted tulips from Whole Foods because it was springtime. I wasn't yet apprised of Lana's history with tulips. Uncannily, my gift might be seen as a reparation of the laceration once imposed on the tulips in Lana's childhood yard, even as I cared for her while the laceration across her chest healed.

Twice a month I would inject shots of Neulasta, an immune cell booster, in Lana's thigh. Now, when I give myself shots of testosterone, Lana feels that she should reciprocate, but this would only compound stress for both of us. I started taking T in 2020. Perhaps it was a midlife crisis or perhaps it was the first time in my life that altering my gender identity passed the threshold from impossibility to possibility. As a child, although my family would tease me about being so boyish that I must want to grow a dick, actually acquiring one was inconceivable. In adolescence it would have been irresponsible to burden my father with personal problems when group subsistence was a priority. In young adulthood I only had healthcare when I was a student, and gender transition or affirmation was precluded by my studies and the multiple low-paying university jobs necessary for survival.

In my current full-time academic job, I witness a younger generation of queers who take their lives into their hands in ways I never could have imagined. At a studio visit, one of my students divulged that they were starting on T. For at least five or ten minutes I could not get words out. I did not have the vocabulary to enter that moment with them. Tears came to me more readily than words.

I am slightly more hip to the trans community now after a friend turned me on to the YouTube videos where twelve-year-olds instruct on how to cope with life while taking T. Charmingly, this is the same demographic that gives primers on how to make titles in Final Cut Pro, a much appreciated intergenerational knowledge sharing. The Facebook group All Trans Men Know Each Other has been entertaining and helpful, though posts come sporadically as people leave Facebook, myself included. Still, during the early phase of the COVID pandemic, their loose solidarity across solitude was a comfort. They humanized and celebrated what has always been shamed in my birth family and country.

Lana and I have not failed to notice the connections between breast cancer and trans medical needs. Women with breast cancer and trans men both undergo breast surgery to save their lives. Before Lana's mastectomy, we solicited tips on drain care and scar reduction from trans masculine friends. For some cancer patients, treatment involves hormone suppression whereas trans folx require hormone supplements, but both communities may suffer from hormone imbalances and may be reliant on a regimen of injections.

To be honest, I dislike injecting myself, and I am not certain I'll need to continue taking T. Gender affirmation can be far less definitive than many cis people believe. Yet each time I practice the ritual of injection, clasping the vial between my thumb and forefinger, I am awed at this tiny tube's vitality. Nearly identical, these vessels can contain vastly different substances: pegfilgrastim, the bone marrow supplement Lana used; testosterone;

mRNA COVID-19 vaccines. These fragile, slim cylinders hold immense privilege. For some, an elixir. Perhaps having had access to such possibility has been enough.

The summer after chemotherapy, under the guise of Lana attending a conference, we went to Banff to celebrate in the Canadian wilderness. The mere sight of Lake Louise, its turquoise surface with fog rising from it like steam, could have cleansing properties, and with close to sixteen hours of daylight, we might reverse any vitamin D deficiency Lana had acquired. Lana bought attractive figure-hugging linen pants, which almost immediately she outgrew. During chemo she lost enough weight that the subway car seating was painful because she had no padding. Although she thought of food incessantly, she never dreamed, as Alice B. Toklas did during the food scarcity of the Occupation, of an oblong silver dish, floating in air, three large slices of ham resting on it. If she had known about the myth of ma lai rút ruột, she might have attributed her insatiable hunger to this demon, and not to epirubicin, the chemotherapy cousin to doxorubicin, the "red devil." But one wouldn't need to be as superstitious as I to be assured that nothing would be left to tempt the nocturnal monster since the hospital recommended flushing twice to avoid any contamination to non-cancer patients. That summer, Lana was quickly restored to her former body mass, and she still regrets that she was only able to wear her new linen pants in the changing room.

In 2012, a month and a half shy of two years after her diagnosis, we spent four months in London where Lana would write her dissertation in earnest. I explored the city, attending art exhibits and often joining her at the Freud Museum and British Library, and would come home with loads of crisp, tart apples, which we both relished despite their imperfect appearance. When we moved from Hampstead to Islington halfway through Lana's residency, every other day she would jog along the Regent's Canal, listening to *The Immortal Life of Henrietta Lacks* and *The Year of Magical Thinking*, contemplating what her body had been through and grappling with how to arrange thoughts into words on a page. She read about how before Gertrude Stein was wheeled into the surgery for stomach cancer from which she would not return alive, the writer asked Alice B. Toklas, "What is the answer?" Finding her partner silent, she followed with, "In that case . . . what is the question?" Lana refrained from referring to this anecdote when she first encountered it during her early research into cancer, but it lurked in her brain as she sought answers to her treatment. How to re-imagine one's body, and one's life as a body, as bodies, when answers are not forthcoming? Stein offers a strategy that Lana and I continue to abide by, one of re-orienting oneself to the practice of seeking questions.

•

When Lana leaves home wearing her red spectacles, she is primed for the constant chorus of: "I love your glasses!" The compliment might come from a person she is sitting in front of on the train or a passerby on the street, or a cashier, a colleague, the doorman in her office building, a street vendor, a friend of a friend, a bus driver, a bartender, ticket taker, doctor, or stranger sitting nearby in the park. Lana's red glasses are not actually red but rather transparent with a red coating. What gives them their distinct flair is the clear plastic crowning that suggests you might catch a glimpse of something through them, and hints at a message that might be meant for you, a secret in hiding.

Eyewear, as Sedgwick points out, is particularly suited to exposing the gap between how one appears to others and how one appears to oneself. More times than I'd like to recount, Lana and I, or just Lana, will be standing in line at a cinema, or at the airport, or at a deli counter, or waiting to be seated at a restaurant, or at a pharmacy, or at a polling station, or at a grocery store, or clothing store, and someone will move ahead of her as if she were not even there. Accustomed to being intentionally or unintentionally under-seen, Lana has had to adjust to the attention her red glasses garner.

They are indeed arresting glasses, and they have fulfilled a function that she has longed to have an object fulfill all her life, though she did not recognize this longing until she possessed them. The reason for her unceasing gratitude to her glasses is that they do the speaking for her. They say, I am bold, I am present, I have presence, I am unafraid of standing out or of what others think or of what styles are in fashion. They are vanguard, they are retro, they are timeless. They fit her face, and suit her so well, which surprises her because she feels that they are everything she is not. They defy her constant sense of invisibility, of being not so much a wallflower as a wall weed, or perhaps simply the wall itself. While hesitation continuously holds her hostage, these glasses make a clear, unambivalent statement. They give her courage, and they allow her to remain silent while speaking volumes.

In his book *Covering*, Kenji Yoshino describes his visit to a haberdashery where he finds a baroque vest with gold lions and cobalt brocade. He aches to try it on, and his trial is met with the shopkeeper's effusive "It becomes you." Yoshino writes, "I realized it did become me, and that I could become it. It did the work outlandish clothes do for us—it drove my invisible difference to the surface and held it there, relieving my psyche of that work." This is precisely the work that Lana's red glasses do for her. Once when she was preparing to give a job talk, I recommended that she forego them, fearing that they would read as too declarative. Plagued by lifelong indecision, Lana occasionally is gripped with decisiveness. She insisted that she must wear the glasses. They were not only a crutch, they presented a concise picture of who she was, better than she thought she would be able to under the pressures of an interview. This assessment proved prescient, as she was offered the job.

Sedgwick writes of her obsession with the white-framed glasses of her beloved friend Michael Lynch, how she had to find the closest thing to a replica as possible and, having found them, how she wore them in Michael's presence, amazed that it was possible for people to tell them apart. She feels this uncanny symmetry or synchronicity or confusion of selves despite her awareness of not only their obvious physical differences but the ways in which whiteness is gendered. The gendering and racializing, even the sizeism-ing (Sedgwick emphasizes her fatness as a visible signifier of difference) that is embedded in profiling people's eyewear, and, by extension, profiling in general, is evident in the constant confusion between Lana and me. Lana and I bear out Sedgwick's fantasy of mimesis, purportedly because we are both Asian, of relatively small build, and gender non-conforming, though Lana leans toward femme, and I move beyond the binary.

There is also the similarity between our names, Lana being contained in Lan Thao. I suppose one might call Lana the joey, the baby kangaroo to my kangaroo. Wikipedia defines a kangaroo word as a word that contains all the letters of one of its synonyms, which is the joey word. For instance, "malign" is the joey word to the kangaroo word "malignant." Often people who see our names in writing simply cannot see them in distinction.

Should this have happened to Sedgwick, she surely would have been delighted. She muses: "When I am with Michael, often suddenly it will be as if we were fused together at a distance of half an inch from the eye." And, yes, there are times when, with pleasure, Lana and I experience ourselves as fused together, but the pleasure in this is in seeing each other and ourselves, seeing each other *in* ourselves, and not in being seen by others as each other. In fact, it is not being seen as separate entities by others that breaks the spell.

Lana spotted her frames at Archangel Antiques on Ninth Street between First and Second Avenues. Entering the curio shop, you took a step or two down from street level and arrived in a narrow room crowded to its tin ceiling with an array of eclectic objects. It felt like Old New York, whatever that means to you. As the Archangel Antiques Facebook page says, "Where else could you buy a taxidermied leopard's head AND a vintage dress from the 1940s?" I chatted with the owner, who was impeccably dressed in a Commes des Garçons jacket that I was coveting. He would be closing up shop after twenty-one years. He was headed to Florida where he hoped to marry his boyfriend. The subject of marriage came up because I was shopping for my own wedding attire. A shirt bedecked with graceful magenta and cadmium orange flowers was calling to the Dapper Dan in me. Lana was fingering antique buttons (apparently, they had over two million of them dating from the Victorian

Era), pocket watches, cufflinks, jewelry, and other collectibles when she uncovered the glasses. Although she had somewhat recently bought a pair of retro black plastic frames, she couldn't resist trying on the red ones. They became her, and she instantly seemed to become them. Nevertheless, she reached for a pair of black frames that were not memorable. I dismissed the staid black as too similar to the ones she already had. As per usual, she needed to be convinced to take home what she most desired. But as Archangel's Yelp page boasts, "If your [*sic*] breathing we will sell you something." I bought a crisp aquamarine pocket square and four buttons that spelled out "L-U-C-K." I would later come back for the shirt, which stayed in my mind after Lana walked out with the red frames in her backpack.

Lana is against marriage, and yet she agreed to enter into the contract of marriage after fourteen years of sharing our lives. We both believe that marriage will not and has not set us free. We never expected it to. As longtime unmarried people who put no trust in the sanctity of the couple form, we are keenly aware of the injustices at the heart of the institution. But it has the power to make some a little less unfree, especially in areas of immigration and healthcare.

For reasons I still cannot fully understand, from an early point in our relationship I yearned to marry Lana or to be married to Lana with a longing that can only compare to my need for caffeine in the morning, every morning. My only explanation is that sometimes we cannot resolve the irresolvabilities of our urges. Perhaps it already felt like a *fait accompli*. I am convinced that we were connected in a past life, perhaps leaving a promise unfulfilled. This may be why we married before it was legal at the federal level, and I therefore acquired a green card through employment and not by marriage, as some might presume.

Differential status marked Lana's and my relationship until I finally obtained a green card after twenty-one years of living and working in the U.S. Prior to this, my time in the U.S. was stitched together from visa to visa while Lana enjoyed the security and privileges of citizenship. Even though Lana has always felt untethered, her citizenship provides the foundation upon which her employment and long-term residence rests. After finding her Thirteenth Street apartment, she stayed there for seven years before reluctantly uprooting herself at my insistence. We're approaching twenty-two years in our Washington Heights apartment. For those of us who have not always enjoyed the world as a welcoming place, a person may serve as buoy to survive the buffets that threaten our ruin. As I was for Lana when she clung to me aboard the dinghy reeling on the South China Sea, so she is for me.

Lana had the opportunity to gaze upon Sedgwick's white glasses when we visited Hal Sedgwick in his West Village apartment. She brought me along because she didn't trust herself to take photographs under pressure. She didn't expect to see Eve Sedgwick's glasses but was captivated when they appeared in her peripheral vision. They were folded and lying on a piece of green silk cloth, maybe one of Eve's scarves, a centerpiece of a small shrine containing a verdigris dragonfly and a Buddha lying prone, a marble standing feminine figure holding a fish by the tail in one hand and a basket in the other, Tibetan Buddhist beads, cymbals, and a singing bowl with wooden mallet. The glasses seemed to be observing the quiet scene. Lana was surprised at how unassuming they looked. They were much thinner than she had imagined them—not at all like patio furniture, as Eve had described Michael's.

Hal unpacked a box of Eve's hats. He then brought out two items that were particularly intriguing: Eve's neck brace and radiation therapy mask. Lana had read about the neck brace, decorated with Cinco de Mayo skeletons, but the mold of Eve Sedgwick's head and shoulders astonished her. It looked like a spectral science fiction effigy. There is something spooky about confronting the outline of a person one has never met, in their absence.

The process of mold making—its materialization of the evacuated body—has long fascinated me. A perfect replica of the face, head, and shoulders, a radiation therapy mask is designed to hold a patient's head in place, secured to the treat-

ment table, so she remains perfectly immobile while radio-
therapy is delivered. With it a radiologist would not have to
try to avoid the heart, as had been offered at our consultation.
A warm, wet sheet of thermoplastic mesh was placed over
Sedgwick's head and shoulders to harden for fifteen minutes.
Purple (more accurately red overscored with blue) crosses or
half crosses presumably mark the therapy targets, three on the
right side, from beneath the chin and moving toward the chest.
A couple of marks on either side of where her jawbone may
have been are just blue. Four circular objects, a little like wash-
ers for minuscule screws, outlined with blue ink, are appended
above the right eyebrow, the left cheek, and two on the chest.
Three circles are missing a circular object inside them: one on
the right check, one at the chin, one below the chin. A label
printed with "Sedgwick, Eve" and a barcode are adhered to the
top of the mold.

Lana felt as if she were facing a part-object—part of a psy-
chic-object-of-love-and-attachment, detached and exerting a
force all the more intense because isolated from the original
object—materialized before her eyes.

Sedgwick falls in love with a gay poet activist wearing patio-
furniture glasses who had just lost his ex-lover to AIDS. Michael, his glasses, and his loss are inseparable from each other
and are together the source of her identification with him.
Lana, a small Asian woman married to an Asian trans person,

strongly identifies with Sedgwick, a fat woman married to a white man. They have both had breast cancer and their right breast removed. Lana's identification with Sedgwick is sparked by Sedgwick's failure to identify as a woman. Having a disease so immediately identified as a woman's disease is alienating for those whose gender identity is not located in the most obvious symbolic body part that is too often equated with womanhood. Illness in general, breast cancer in particular, can put into question one's gender identity, can alter the already tenuous image that one has of one's self, and produce an even larger gap, a yawning chasm even, between how one imagines oneself and how one is perceived.

After my dad's funeral I took home his hole-ridden cardigan, his aroma still carried in its weave. When I wear it, it molds around my shoulders as if I am being held. Lana likes to borrow my sweaters and hoodies for this reason, because objects, both material and psychic, impart something to us that can feel like love.

Although I had been proposing marriage to Lana for many years prior to her diagnosis with breast cancer, it was this that tipped it over for me, to know that my presence in the hospital, should there be a future need, would not be questioned. Sedgwick defines "queer" as a tendency. I want us to be queer for each other, to tend to each other, to care for one another on our own terms.

We chose a spot in our neighborhood park where we could see "our" bridge, the one others named after George Washington. It was a very windy day. All the photos that were taken freeze people's hair in curious, impossible formations, except for Lana, who sensibly wore a 1920s-style hat that was a gift to herself during chemo. The public legal sanction of our togetherness sealed something; it is, after all, a recognizable ritual, an official contract. We cleaned up for the occasion. I wore the fanciful Archangel shirt and, for some reason, Lana decided to go without her red glasses that day. Maybe she didn't need them because she knew that, unlike others who stop her on the street to say they love her glasses, I don't need her glasses to profess my love.

After he passed, I noticed in my dad's bookcase a thesaurus he had purchased for the ESL classes that my sisters and I took when we arrived in Canada. I believe I was the only one who ever used it. I flipped to the opening page, which warns: "How to Use This Book—A Word of Caution." My adolescent self had circled "denotation" and underlined "connotation." The author clarifies that "a denotation of *home* is 'where a person resides': the connotation of *home* may include such emotional overtones as 'warmth, comfort, affection, good food,' and so forth." I learned the denotation of home as a teenage immigrant who suffered a radical displacement from her childhood birthplace, and would continue to underscore its denotative meaning as I moved from one residence to another. I did not fully experience the connotative dimensions of "home" until I found it with Lana, and I mean "found" in both its senses of discovery and construction. My home is with Lana and hers with me. The word "music" that appears on the floor plan we sketched when deciding to purchase our co-op, that neither of us remembers inscribing on the napkin, that remains a mystery because neither of us is particularly musical, fortuitously describes the connotative character of the home that Lana and I have forged in concert with the overtones of warmth, comfort, affection, good food, and so forth.

VI.

THE WAR

I was born amid what has since been deemed the turning point of the Vietnam War, though "watershed" may be a more appropriate descriptor. Chaos, violence, death, and destruction are precisely not contained within a point. Tết is the colloquial abbreviation of Tết Nguyên Đán, the Festival of the First Morning of the First Day, commemorated on the first day of the Lunar New Year. In 1968 this was January 31. If you ask Google how long the Tet Offensive lasted, it will tell you twenty-six days. But if you ask when the Tet Offensive ended, it will come up with September 23, 1968. The simplicity of the answer is contingent upon how one phrases the question. As Stein resolved, in the absence of definitive answers, all we can rely upon are questions. By some accounts the Tet Offensive was halted on February 24 when the South Vietnamese flag was raised at the Citadel in Huế, although fighting persisted until nearly the end of September. Guerilla strikes were still common in the Mekong Delta town of Mỹ Tho when I was born.

The day after my birth, NBC News reporter Frank McGee remarked, "We must decide whether it is futile to destroy Vietnam in an effort to save it." McGee was echoing a widely reported statement from a U.S. official about Bến Tre, the site of my grandmother's home, that has since become emblematic of U.S. militarism and imperialism: "It became necessary to destroy the town to save it." Soon after my birth, when bombs were unleashed on our home, everybody ran to the shelter, leaving me in my crib. In the morning, my family emerged and found shrapnel scattered all around my bassinet and even underneath it. According to the family lore, I slept through it all. By the time I was twelve years old I might have died four times, but, somehow, I was always protected.

For Tết, we would all get new clothes, and on three occasions we even went to a photography studio in Sài Gòn for a formal family portrait. Hair slicked down on either side of an arrow-straight part, I stood stiffly in my 100 percent polyester dress, restraining my hands from itching around the collar. I was properly chastened by past experiences when my mom would issue a reprimand if I squirmed too much for her liking. The only other studio photograph I had seen was of my parents' wedding, in which both my parents gleamed with carefree youth. And then when my mom and youngest sister joined us in Canada, after we'd escaped and could sponsor them, we splurged on a Sears family photo at the newly opened Metrotown in Burnaby, British Columbia. They were having a grand opening sale. We also have photos that my dad took at my grandparents' house with a medium-format camera he may have borrowed or rented. My grandmother, in formal *áo dài*, is positioned with both hands outspread on her lap, the classic posture demonstrating that the subject has preserved each of her digits, a sign of good health and privilege. A roll of Super 8 mm film that my sister Trang transferred to video shows the extended family awkwardly standing around, getting ready to arrange ourselves as if we were posing for a photograph. Everyone's movements are jerky because the film was shot at silent speed in Kodachrome saturated color.

The night before going to Grandma's house I was always too excited to sleep. Bleary eyed, I would climb into the Toyota with my sisters, and then we'd stop at my aunt's to pick up more kids, so there might be as many as twenty kids packed into the car. On the way there my sister Thu and I would sit between Mom's legs in the front, and on the way home I once had to stand, grabbing ahold of the driver's seat from behind—sometimes poking my dad's neck when the car jolted over a pothole—to keep myself from lurching onto the pile of my cousins who were squeezed into the backseat.

My grandfather was very strict about who would be the first person to cross the threshold of his dwelling on the first day of the new year. If their name was Bright Shining Fortune Bringing, then he would invite them in. None of our names were auspicious enough. We would tumble out of the car and wade through the red and white paper littering the grounds, the detritus of firecrackers detonated to chase away evil spirits that might cast a bad omen upon the new year. Deafening explosions took the place of the grinding sound of rice mill machinery that typically ran at all hours behind my grandparents' house. On Tết, the sweet smell of rice being milled, mixed with the odor of diesel that fueled the machine, was overpowered by the aroma of slow-cooked pork belly with egg stew. We also made a point of eating bitter melon soup so that the bitterness of hardship would pass us over, as the Vietnamese name for the melon suggests.

Both my maternal and paternal grandparents cultivated yellow apricot blossoms that bloomed just before the new year. I would stretch up to tug off one of the red envelopes of lucky money that adorned the shrub's branches. Before visiting Grandma's, I marveled at the bonsai-style ornamental plants arranged in the Sài Gòn market that had made their way up the Delta by boat. I do not know if my second sister, Mai, was named after this plant, which we call *cây mai* or *hoa mai*. I felt close to the legend of Hoa Mai because the girl dreamed of becoming a hunter like her father. She excelled with a bow and arrow, and even a sword. When a snake monster terrorized her village, father and daughter set out to vanquish the beast. Her mother gave her a shirt dyed with turmeric so her daughter would blaze like the sun. The warrior beheaded the serpent with a single strike of her sword, but with its dying breath, it thrashed its tail around the girl's neck and suffocated her. Taking pity on the mourning family, the Kitchen God entreated the Jade Emperor to give permission for the girl to rejoin them for nine days. Impressed with the girl's heroic sacrifice, the King of Heaven allowed her to visit Earth from December 29 of the lunar calendar until the night of the seventh day of the Lunar New Year. Eventually Hoa Mai was transformed into a tree glowing with golden blossoms, which is why Southern Vietnamese celebrate the new year with *mai* flowers.

When I came to Canada, I recognized that the evergreen trees lined up for sale in a high-school parking lot carried symbolic value similar to our beloved *Ochna integerrima* shrubs. Watching *A Charlie Brown Christmas* on an old TV given to us by our new landlord, I was touched by the solitary ornament clinging to a sad pine branch. I had only seen black-and-white television in Sài Gòn, and I was struck by how the lonely red globe vibrated on the screen. Four decades later, I would replicate the humble tree at the site of another mill where Lana and I do not celebrate Christmas but shelter an abundance of orphaned branches and an enduring affection for *Peanuts*.

My dad had commissioned a local welder to make bikes for my older sisters that had their names engraved on the gear covers. Maybe it was because their names were carved into the aluminum that I wasn't to inherit one of their bikes when I reached the age and size to begin riding. As the fifth of six sisters, most everything I owned had been handed down to me, except the stamps I bought for my burgeoning collection with the money my mom gave me to buy *bánh mì* for breakfast. My sense of ownership and achievement arrived with a beautiful bronze bike that my dad had likely purchased in Singapore.

My bike was special, different from my sisters' models, because it folded and boasted a passenger seat. I could transport not only myself but others as well. I was especially proud when I mastered a trick of moving from my seat to the passenger saddle without even stopping. Biking afforded me a sense of autonomy and agency. After falling time and time again when my sister released her grip, that moment when I first felt myself moving forward as if set free, assurance took over like a reflex. Pedals spinning, wind streaking across my face, I gripped my handlebars with the conviction that I could power myself, that I could propel myself somewhere, maybe into the future.

Our first home in Sài Gòn was at 111 Triệu Đà. My dad said this was a lucky number. Triệu Đà is the name of a former Chinese general who founded the kingdom of Nam Việt in 207 BCE. But as a child I mistook Triệu Đà for Bà Triệu, the revolutionary heroine who, riding an elephant, battled the Chinese. I would imagine myself as the commander Triệu, my bike as the elephant. Bà Triệu was not so much an icon for me because of her nationalism or patriotism but because of her defiance of a passive femininity. She was valorized in a tradition of Vietnamese women warriors, preceded, for example, by the Trưng sisters who also fought on elephants against the Chinese. When the Communists took over the government, Triệu Đà Alley became Ngô Quyền, commemorating a Vietnamese leader who defeated the Chinese after a thousand years of their rule and established an independent Vietnamese kingdom. I never had to get used to the name change because around 1974, when I was six years old, my family moved from 111 Triệu Đà to 304 Trần Hoàng Quân, a three-story house.

Mounting whispers began to signal the end of the war. My dad and uncles huddled around the radio, listening to *Voice of America* and the BBC broadcast in Vietnamese. My uncles would come and go, #8 and #9 were in the military, and #3 was a general or high officer of some sort. Uncle #10 was too young to serve, and uncle #6 had died in the Tet Offensive. My mom prepared, for each of her five daughters, a shopping bag that we were responsible for if anything happened. Her sixth daughter, my little sister Thy, would have been too young to carry her own bag. Each bag was made of plastic mesh and contained a kilo of rice; 500 đồng, which may have been worth about one U.S. dollar; and a copy of our birth certificate. The sacks lined the wall in the garage. If we needed to run, we were to grab our bags. I never touched mine. I don't think I was aware of what it contained. I only knew it was there and it was mine. My mom clutched the handle and my wrist for emphasis, repeating, "This is your bag."

On April 30, 1975, we watched from our balcony terrace as tanks drove down the street flying a half red, half blue flag centered with a golden star. Stunned, we witnessed the same red-and-blue flag being raised by our neighbor, confirming what we'd never suspected, that she was undergound Việt Cộng. This was the first time I had seen this flag, which was quickly replaced by a uniform red field symbolizing a unified North and South, still centered with a gold star. It was also the first time I had seen a tank. It occurred to me then that this was where I'd stood when I glimpsed a man with salt-and-pepper hair, whom I yearned to become, elegantly riding his bicycle on the street where these tanks were now lumbering forward. An image of erotic aspiration was crushed beneath metal treads. My mom broke my reverie, calling us inside because gunshots were being fired to announce the Communist victory, and we were in danger of being hit by a stray bullet. My uncles shook their heads, gravely pondering that our house at 304, with its address corresponding to the 30th of April, would forever commemorate the Fall of Saigon. This was why the Communist government was so determined to take our house, and why my mom could not hang onto it after my dad, four older sisters, and I left Việt Nam in 1980. But the officials were bitterly disappointed in the empty shell we left behind. Everything of value was sold save for my parents' divan which was transported to my grandma's house and then taken into the custody of one of my uncles when she passed away.

304 was a rowhouse whose roof and attic were connected to all the other houses on the block. The center of the house was open, so from the ground-floor kitchen smoke could rise past the second floor and bathing area to be released through a retractable skylight in the roof that was operated by pulleys. This contraption fascinated me, although it leaked during the rainy season. We didn't live there long enough for me to tire of it. My dad had designed the skylight partly because my room didn't have an outside window. From my bed I could crane my head and gaze at the pink sky swarming with bats as the sun set. I was in awe of the fiery sky churning with black and traced the swirls to the eaves where what seemed like hundreds of pouches hung.

My room had an interior window that faced the big bedroom where Mai, Thao, and Thu slept. I made toy guns out of four chopsticks and rubber bands. I don't know who taught me how to make them, possibly a neighbor, or I may have taught myself. We would shoot paper bullets at each other through the openings between our rooms until Mom had enough of our giggles and shouts and ordered us to sleep.

With the Fall of Saigon to the Communists, suddenly the old 500 đồng had the value of one new đồng. Food was rationed and there was no meat. We were encouraged to grow our own vegetables because of the food shortage. I grew tomatoes from seed because Uncle Hồ told us to, but the ducklings and chicks we still had at the time ate all my seedlings. People were forced to become enterprising. I heard my dad and uncles climb up to the attic and return lugging burlap bags loaded with bats that they would deep fry and chomp on like chicken wings, the Vietnamese post-war bar food.

Soon white rice was replaced with brown rice and then sweet potatoes. My mom would send me and my older sister Thu to sell sweet potatoes on the street. This show of poverty was meant for the neighbors. Since my dad had worked for the previous government as a civil engineer, we needed to display our fallen state even though my family would never escape suspicion. Business was poor because sweet potatoes were everywhere. There were so many sweet potatoes you couldn't eat them fast enough, and you had no idea what else to do with them. Why would anyone want to buy more of them? Thu and I would sit on a little stool with our little table topped with a pyramid of sweet potatoes, our clothes and our inventory collecting dust. I spent the time grinding my name in the dirt with a stick, tightly rolling paper bullets for my arsenal, and complaining with Thu about the dearth of customers. Thu and I gradually ended up eating all the sweet potatoes ourselves.

One day I rode to the market with my sister Mai on my passenger seat. Crammed with stalls, the market wasn't accessible to a bike, so I waited outside with it. A woman called out, "Hey you!" and accused me of beating up someone, her daughter or brother or some other kid.

I was appalled and replied, "I didn't beat anyone up!" She then convinced me to take her somewhere to sort all this out. I knew I hadn't wronged anyone. In fact, I was the one feeling wronged and misrepresented. I set out to prove my integrity as the daughter of a teacher. We were taught to be careful of strangers, but my pride was pricked.

The woman sat on the back seat, and I rode her to a deserted park. I can still picture its overgrown fern coverage. I had never been to this part of Sài Gòn before. She glanced around and snapped, "Well, they're not here. Why don't I borrow your bike and go find them? You just wait here. I'll be right back." I agreed and enjoined her to bring back the liar so that I would not lose face. She took off, never to return. I waited and waited.

In the back of my schoolbook a section instructed you to ask a police officer if you ever needed help. I followed my textbook's advice and found a police officer who was riding his bicycle. I sputtered out my story, "I don't know where I am, and I need to get home." Now it was my turn to be in the passenger seat. His bike didn't have a footrest in the back, so I accidentally rested my heel on the spokes. I think I saw the blood, but I was so distraught I didn't feel anything. I just wanted to get home. When we arrived, my mom and fifth aunt ran out to greet us. They thanked the policeman and gave him some money. I still hadn't registered that I had been tricked.

My mom turned to me and demanded, "What happened? Where have you been? Where's your bike?"

"Just wait, wait, wait," I cried. "Don't worry, I'll tell you about it. Let me talk, let me talk."

After I recounted the tale my dad said to my mom, "Don't get too angry. Don't punish her. We could have lost her. We're lucky that they just wanted the bike." We no longer had the Toyota because gas was too expensive. My dad had bought a motorcycle, and the next day he took my mom and me to the scene of the crime. The place was completely abandoned, and they understood then that my throat could have been slit or I could have disappeared. The aftermath of the war spawned a lot of illegal activity—scams, sex trafficking, kidnapping for child labor, and black magic. They were discussing whether or not I might have been hypnotized, but since I vividly recollected so many details, they dispensed with that hypothesis. It wasn't until then, in that unkempt lot that looked like the setting for a ghost story, that I apprehended from my parents' hushed tones that I would never ride my beloved bronze bike again.

With this blow, and the revelation of our underground Việt Cộng neighbor, I was being trained in distrust. The neighborhood watch had already started, and they taught you in school that no one could be trusted, not even your own family. This would prove to be true, but not because anyone reported disloyalty to the Communist government. I would discover that my father kept a mistress. The secretary who had always treated me so nicely when I went to visit my father at work became pregnant with a boy, or so fortune tellers foretold, and my dad wanted a son so badly he was willing to expose his affair. In the end, it turned out that the child was not even his, but an unconscious seed had been planted in the furrow of his betrayal. I nurtured the wish that I could be that boy.

For a few weeks after my bike was stolen, I couldn't walk or run around because of my injured heel. I still have the scar that reminds me of my lost treasure. To console me as I lay bedridden, my fifth aunt, who was a former police officer, let me play with her revolver lighter, which I coveted. When you pulled the trigger, it sparked a flame. She drained the lighter fluid so I wouldn't set fire to my mosquito netting. I whiled away the hours cocking and releasing the trigger, soothed by the gentle click that remotely resembled the clicking of the spokes as my wheels turned, a melody I would miss in the coming bike-less years.

When my dad went to reeducation camp, I don't think he suspected that it would be like prison. Men of his stature wanted to prove themselves to the new government, and in fact when he was initially called to report to the Party, they told him he could go home. He voluntarily returned to explicate his title and position to the inexperienced Party members who were from the rural North and had no idea what "civil engineer" meant. This time when he came home, he packed a bag and bid us goodbye. When we next set eyes on him, at least six months later, his pudgy belly had disappeared. He was half the weight of his former self even though he had not been forced to do hard labor. His wrist was bare, an arresting sight because every man in Việt Nam wore a wristwatch, unless he was a laborer. I found out afterwards that he had sold his watch to get supplements at the commissary.

Every year after the war ended our prospects grew more and more grim. Escape became the only option. My dad tried eight or nine times. My eldest sister Trang tried fourteen times. I made two attempts, one when I was eleven and then again the following year. I don't know where she got the money, perhaps she sold the last of her jewelry, but before we left my mom presented my dad with a new Rolex, which he would need for navigation.

I remember vomiting until there was nothing more to come up. My sister Mai leaned next to me. I must have vomited on her. Dad had positioned himself between his two youngest, with me on one side and Thu on the other. We were in the lower level of a fishing boat. As the waves beat down, water crept along the plywood that shut us in and rained on us. We were drenched in freezing salt water, our backs arched along the curve of the boat. Mom, who had stayed home with Thy, had made tamarind balls with ginger and sugar to settle the stomach. It was all we had to eat, and all we had to puke up. Trang carried them in her bag, and they were passed from sister to sister. For our escape, we were to carry nothing that could incriminate us, that could identify us to others. Only Dad and Trang held bare necessities. The sacks that had lined the garage were meant for an emergency during the war. I had no bag with me. I had nothing, not even pockets.

Through bile-colored haze, I recall that at one point someone opened the hatch, and we were allowed to crawl out to the very front of the boat. All I could see was a wave higher than anything I had ever seen in my life, taller than a tree or house or building. It consumed my field of vision in shimmering black. I clambered back as quickly as I could, terrified that the mammoth wave would crush me. I don't know why I would have chosen to peer out into that horrific storm. Possibly to get some relief from the putrid stench that engulfed us below deck. We were all certain we would die. Once the sailors above called down for my dad because he could speak some English, but he didn't go up. He said that if we died, we would all die together.

By morning the sea had calmed, and the horizon became a flat line. A school of dolphins swam by, mesmerizing me. As we drifted, I would ask my dad if we were headed toward the mountains, and he would reply that there weren't any mountains. I must have mistaken the clouds for mountains.

A white flag was raised. My sisters had hand copied from a dictionary all the flags of the world onto loose pages that my dad slipped into his notebook. I'm not sure why they didn't just tear out the illustrations, but this is how I learned that S.O.S. stands for "save our souls." When it seemed that our flag's message would not be answered, a Polish tanker came into view.

I was small enough to be hoisted aboard. Others had to climb up a rope. A man, maybe he was the captain, took me to his quarters. I don't know why I was chosen. Perhaps because my dad had offered me up for adoption. I thought it was strange, though not sexual, that the man bathed me. I must have smelled awful. He had big, hairy, white hands that put me into his bunkbed. I fell asleep alone, that I know.

When I woke up, I saw those hands playing cards with other men sitting around and talking. Someone brought me a cup of Lipton tea with lemon. I had never tasted Lipton tea before. It was also strange. I wanted to leave and be with my family. In school we had been learning English, but I only knew three verbs: to be, to have, and to do. I did not know the English words for "father" or "sister." I did not know the English word for "go" or "leave." All I could do was put together "I am" and then point to the door. I knew the noun "door" and kept repeating the phrase, "I am door," and pointing to the exit. At first the man shook his head and said "no." Everyone was confused. I think they eventually understood because somehow I ended up back with my family. Years later, Trang asked me if anything had happened in the cabin. I did not feel violated. He may have put something in the tea, but I was so disoriented, how was I to know?

The Poles returned us to Việt Nam, but they didn't give up my dad. He wedged himself into the space between four oil barrels. My sisters and I were brought to jail. We told them everything we knew, but, by design, we didn't know anything. We only knew not to give our real names. I don't remember what my fake name was. Being the oldest, Trang took the fall for all of us. She had to stay in jail for maybe a month. After that she was even more determined to leave. She was approaching military age and would be sent out to sweep the fields for mines.

As children we were told never to buy water that was sold on the street because it was unhygienic. But when we were released, we were so thirsty we bought a single bag for all four of us to share. Thao scolded Thu and me to save some for Mai. We got on a bus and then walked the remaining miles to our aunt's house because we had no more money. Our aunt took one look at the grimy, stinking, barefoot children standing before her, pulled us in, and shut the door.

We didn't call ahead because we didn't know who or what to trust, including the phones. We ate and probably bathed, and then our aunt gave us money to take another bus back to Sài Gòn. From the bus station the four of us piled into a cyclo that took us home. My aunt must have called our mom because she was waiting for us and quickly brought us into the house. Nothing was said. There was nothing to say.

I don't remember my dad hugging us or saying goodbye when he went to hide, but later Trang said that he did. Apparently, the Polish ship docked in Sài Gòn, and he waited until late at night before he climbed down the anchor line and swam into the harbor. Sài Gòn Port in 1979 was no doubt disgusting, teeming with oil, trash, and sewage. I guess he hailed a cyclo driver, who must have known he escaped from something but never reported him. I didn't hear Dad when he crept home at dawn. All I know is that when we woke up, he was there.

A cloak of sadness enveloped our house. At night I could hear my parents' low whispers because my room was right next to theirs. The words were unintelligible, but the tone was grave with anxiety crisping its edges. Over the next six months my dad studied naval navigation and maps of the sea. He made a compass. I don't know how much any of the escape attempts had cost, but I knew that gold was the only currency that could buy your escape, and we had expended our reserve.

When Trang returned from jail her hatred for the Communist Party had only grown. We never talked about it, but I imagine that she was threatened with hard-labor camp. She was intent on getting out by any means. Trips were planned and the boat would leave before its scheduled departure because it was already at or beyond capacity. Trips were called off for fear of being found out. Either way you would lose your money. Determined not to literally miss the boat again, Trang went a day or two before the appointed hour and secured a spot on a boat that was rescued by a German ship that was chartered by Deutsche Not-Ärzte Komitee (German Emergency Physicians Committee). Aboard the ship a film crew was making a documentary about the Vietnamese boat people. The cameraperson essentially adopted Trang into his family for the next five years, and made a 1987 film in which she was the central character: *Trang: Fremd in Deutschland* (*Trang: Foreign in Germany*). Trang would end up spending her adult life in Germany editing films, and she lives in Cologne to this day.

My dad and Mai were supposed to be on that boat that took Trang. The opportunities for escape were fast closing. My dad, Mai, Thao, Thu, and I left Việt Nam before the end of the school year. My mom remembers that it was March, her memory aided by a Vietnamese rhyme: *Tháng ba bà già đi biển* (The month of March, the old lady goes to the sea). But if my mom is the "old lady," she did not yet go to sea. Mom and Thy stayed behind again so that there would be a home to return to if anything went wrong. My memory tells me it was probably closer to May, as the cicadas were coming out. Before our departure, I bequeathed my cherished stamp collection to Thy, because I would fail in my duty to teach her how to swim and ride a bike as my sisters had done for me.

This time we weren't to be stowaways. The boat was to be filled only with extended family. My mom's side of the family were fishermen. Somebody had already found a boat that was seaworthy. Everyone chipped in to buy the boat and supplies: rice, fish sauce, dry goods, oil, and water. The weather was far better than on our earlier attempt, but still we ran out of gas before we reached our destination. A Malaysian boat was spotted and flagged down. The fishermen asked for all our valuables in exchange for enough fuel to reach land. They gave us some water and pointed us in the direction of the port of Terengganu. The men took off their watches. My dad got to keep his Rolex because we needed one timepiece. We'd been at sea for five nights and four days and had traveled 503 nautical miles from Sài Gòn.

I didn't witness our actual arrival because I couldn't see from below deck. But I knew it was daytime when we approached the shores of Malaysia. Dad was the only one who could speak English, so he was our official interpreter. Subdued voices descended from above, and then eventually we emerged from the boat and were taken to an abandoned house nearby.

It was roughly whitewashed limestone, small but quite beautiful. There was no furniture inside, so we just huddled there waiting. Thus began the refugee's primary activity, which is to wait. We were to wait in line for the well, to use the toilet, to pick up rations, to be processed, for ferries bearing supplies, for the arrival of letters, for an interview, for an approval for resettlement.

The Malaysian army came to pick us up in a military vehicle, the kind with a cloth cover on top. They transported us to barracks with bunk beds where we slept overnight. Then they put us on a boat to Pulau Bidong, the island camp where we stayed for four or five months.

The Malaysian officials instructed newly arrived refugees to squat in formation on the beach. We waited as the sun beat down on us, sucking the moisture from our parched lips. The song "Biển Nhớ (The Sea Remembers)" played over the PA system, as it was to play every time refugees arrived and departed.

Ngày mai em đi (Tomorrow I leave)

Biển nhớ tên em gọi về . . . (The sea remembers your name, calling you back . . .)

The rhythm of the music mimics the onrushing and receding of sea waves that, like memory, come and go. The impetus to depart is withheld by a call to return. As I listened to those lyrics, I was overcome with a sense of loss; I had no idea when or if I would see my mom and little sister again; I would not be able to add to the stamp album my dad had gifted me; I would not mop the ceramic floor of Trang's top-floor bedroom so that I could have the privilege of sleeping on it with her; I might never again stare at the clouds through the skylight of our three-story house; I might not sweep the yard at my grandma's house ever again. The mangos would grow heavy without us to keep them from falling to the ground. I recalled the theft of my bronze bike, the gash left behind when something beloved is made forever irretrievable, but I'm not certain that at that moment my mind could compass the magnitude of my loss, of all our losses.

I turned my attention to the sand clinging to my toes. The code for our escape was "going to visit Grandpa." If anyone asked where we were going, we were visiting Grandpa, who we all knew was no longer alive. Although it had been an ordeal to get here, our grueling journey "to visit Grandpa" was still not over. We didn't know when we would arrive at a safe and permanent home or where in the world it would be. We didn't know how or when we might be reunited with Mom and Thy or if we would ever see Trang again. To visit Grandpa was to visit the spirit world—not to die, but to travel somewhere that was beyond imagination, that was so foreign to my life thus far that I couldn't conceive of it.

Re-orienting to land was a process. The motion sickness I had experienced at sea carried forward. The pull of gravity had shifted; I was unmoored and could not regain my sense of stability for several days. Perhaps some of this disorientation has never left me. I may have felt nauseous because I was dehydrated and undernourished. The ground beneath me no longer felt secure. The expectation of support could no longer be taken for granted. Though I was conscious of my legs, I may have felt like those who suffer from phantom limb syndrome, cut off from the functionality of their appendages, yet still enduring the pain of separation.

Thao chided me, "Just grow up!" when I couldn't stop crying and was so discombobulated that I couldn't help with the chores. She accused me of becoming a burden to Dad. Thu, who was closest to me in age and my best friend growing up, was also having trouble adjusting. We linked our arms and wandered off to weep together and commiserate about our "evil older sister."

Pulau Bidong, which translates into English as Turtle Island, is one square kilometer. In June 1979 it held 40,000 refugees. It may have peaked at 60,000, and it was estimated to be the most heavily populated place on Earth at that time.

A very long wooden jetty juts out from the shore, reaching toward the sea. I saw a photograph of the jetty from 2002 where only eight of the supporting beams remained standing, and the wooden walkway had completely eroded away. Since the camp closed in 1991, nature and time reclaimed that humble bridge from ship to shore. When Lana and I returned to Pulau Bidong in 2009 the jetty had been rebuilt, perhaps by the Universiti Malaysia Terengganu, which has a research station on the island, or the Terengganu state government, which is planning an underwater gallery. The new jetty, painted pristine white, glared in the beating sun, its terra-cotta roof absorbing the harsh rays where refugees once waited, squatting and exposed. A jetty, for Lana, could only bring to mind Chris Marker's twenty-eight-minute 1963 experimental film *La Jetée*, composed almost entirely of still photographs. I, too, was taken with Marker's film when I saw it in graduate school, although the jetty at Pulau Bidong has little in common with the jetty at Orly airport, the center of Marker's black-and-white science fiction imagining. Nevertheless, *La Jetée* reverberates with my experience in ways I had not considered until this very moment of writing. In Marker's apocalyptic vision of time travel an image is seared into memory, igniting a desire to return to the past, and ultimately conveying the impossibility of such an achievement.

Marker's narration intones: "Moments to remember are just like other moments. They are only made memorable by the scars they leave." The crucial moment in *La Jetée* takes place on a jetty on a hot Sunday before a war, but it is an instant that is simultaneously observed after that war. What day of the week was it when I set foot on that wooden jetty at Pulau Bidong? Was it a Sunday? Would I be marked by this image of my childhood, would it forever haunt me? There at the end of this jetty, "my jetty," which was baked in a "frozen sun," as was the jetty in *La Jetée*, I shared with Marker's time traveler the wish to return to a time before the war, which for me would be before my own birth. I, too, was imprisoned in a camp and a visitor to an unfamiliar territory, who seemed to be out of joint with the whir of activity around me.

Here on the shore, I cocked my head at the horizon line where the sea met the sky, which was blurry and askew. Distant objects had always been somewhat out of focus for me. I would not be prescribed glasses for my nearsightedness until we reached Canada. When I put on my oversized two-toned plastic frames, the edges of the world were sharp for the first time, and leaves popped with a vibrant emerald green. The images that appeared before my eyes were like those of the time traveler in *La Jetée*, "a real bedroom . . . real birds . . . real graves" in peacetime, a world of richness. "Fabulous materials everywhere—glass, plastic, velvet." But in that weary moment crouching on the beach, I had no idea that Canada lay on the horizon. In Sài Gòn, I hadn't had a clear picture of my future. I only knew that people told me I had no future there. They didn't tell me what my future might be nor why the West seemed to hold its keys. My twelve-year-old mind dreamed of an endless supply of toys, Legos galore, an abundance of Petit Ecolier cookies, and grapes, which my dad had once bought for me when I was sick. This fantasy would cruelly mock my reality.

The island currency was U.S. dollars. Just as in Việt Nam and elsewhere in what was once called the Third World, you went to a jeweler to sell your gold in exchange for U.S. dollars. Everybody continued their trade in the local economy of the refugee camp. A whole system that the community established occupied about two city blocks of habitable space. There was a hospital, though fortunately none of my family needed it. There was a Buddhist temple and Christian churches up on a steep hill. A school was being built, but it hadn't started yet, so my schooling was on hiatus until we went to Canada.

Initially we were assigned a small hut. Behind it stood a baker's oven where we could buy fresh baguettes that were delicious. Before daylight, at 3 or 4 A.M., I heard the bakers beginning work, and then at 5 or 6 A.M., the aroma of fresh bread lured us out of bed. This shack was too cramped for our family of six: my dad, three sisters, me, and my dad's nephew from my third aunt who had a family of his own but had left Việt Nam by himself.

When we arrived on the island, someone recognized my sister Thao and called out her name. They said they were leaving the island and asked if we wanted their house. This is how we inherited a house the size of my bedroom in Sài Gòn. The dirt floors were worn shiny and packed down from so many feet treading across them.

By "house" I mean a structure made with corrugated metal that thundered when it rained. We were lucky that our roof didn't leak. I heard of other huts that let in rain and rats, and of people who slept under the canopy of trees and would wake up sticky with dried sap. Thao's friend's family had collected fallen tree branches, latticed them together, and placed layers and layers of flattened corrugated cardboard boxes on top as mattresses. My dad and cousin slept on hammocks. Once we were approved to resettle in Canada and were moved to the transfer station at Sungai Besi, I slept with Thu on the top bunk of a bunk bed. The mattress was probably a couple of inches thick, but it felt so luxurious it was like sleeping on clouds.

On the island we had to fetch water from the well, but we had our own outdoor shower stall in the back. We tried to keep a little garden by the side of the house, but I don't think we were very successful. Other people who had been there for years had managed to grow bean sprouts and sold them in the illegal market.

Every two weeks the ferry would bring food, supplies, and mail. A horn or tune signaled that an announcement would come over the PA system. Everyone stopped to listen. There would be news and a list of who had mail. The whole island grew hushed as the names of those who had letters were read out loud. Even as a child I felt a kind of reverence in those moments. For all the names that were being read out, there were names that had not been read out. The silence of those unnamed was palpable.

Most of the announcements were mundane, directing you where to line up for groceries: Tang, instant noodles, canned sardines, canned corn, and canned red beans. I couldn't eat instant noodles and sardines for years afterwards, but I still love to eat corn with a spoon straight out of a can. Lana was appalled when she first saw me take a can opener to a can of corn and dig in a spoon.

An ex-military man was stationed across from us. He had a big house. It was actually the same size as ours, but we were six and he was one. He had been waiting for resettlement a long time, so he was bored and had stockpiled a hoard of canned goods. From time to time, he would build a bonfire and throw his cans in. One by one they would explode. That was his entertainment. Now and again as we were washing dishes or cooking or eating, we would hear a loud bang, followed by his guffaws. None of us said anything. We kept our distance and went about our business.

My dad was always occupied with some sort of service or another. He was educated and could translate. My older sisters did the cooking as they had at home. I held a knife with my left hand, which is considered bad luck, so the expert chefs would criticize and relegate me to doing the dishes. On the island my job was to dig holes in the back of the house for emergencies. In daylight my sisters and I would trek out to the row of outdoor toilets, but it was too far to walk at night, and it wasn't safe for a girl to go alone. The succession of stalls made of corrugated metal reeked because there was no running water. The local name for the latrine was *Lăng Bác*, which is the nickname for Hồ Chí Minh's mausoleum. Everyone enjoyed doling out the ultimate disrespect of shitting on Hồ Chí Minh's final resting place.

Although we had a flushable toilet in Sài Gòn, my grandmother, aunts, and uncles lived in the country without running water. Their toilet was a hut that was built over a pond swimming with fish that fed off feces. It was quite pleasant to feel the air tickling your bare bottom. You could see my sixth uncle's grave if you looked out, not directly, but to the side of the outhouse. He faced the pond. When you needed to go, and someone asked where you were headed, you would respond, "I'm going to visit uncle #6." We all liked hanging out by my uncle's grave because fruit trees grew nearby, bearing fragrant rambutan and star fruit.

Aside from the primitive living conditions, one of the biggest adjustments for any refugee is the obliteration of privacy. We didn't have any locks. I don't know how my dad kept anything valuable from being stolen. Of course, as far as I knew all we had was my dad's Rolex and a little cash. He didn't tell us where he hid certain things, and I didn't ask. At least we had our own house with a backyard to relieve ourselves. At Sengai Besi, the transfer station, everything was communal. Bunk beds lined the perimeter of the co-ed bedroom, and faucets lined the perimeter of the bathroom. You would take your shower facing the wall in a dim open space. Bathing at the camp I beheld women's naked bodies for the first time. I had never seen pubic hair. I was twelve years old and as bare down there as the lightbulbs dangling above. Confounded, I thought, *Why do they have* that *when I have nothing*? I didn't dare ask even my sisters. Breasts didn't surprise me as much as pubic hair. Nothing prepared me for pubic hair. Decades later when Lana and I went to a spa in Taiwan we entered a dimly lit room, barren save a row of shower heads and faucets in front of which naked women squatted on plastic stools dousing their heads with water, and I exclaimed that it reminded me of a refugee camp. The spa was slightly fancier.

Despite the hardships, uncertainties, and dramatic upheaval, I went on being a kid, and therefore reveled in the one thing I had always taken the greatest pleasure in aside from riding my bike—swimming at the beach. Before the war ended, we would take family vacations at Vũng Tàu, a seaside city a couple of hours drive south of Sài Gòn. I first encountered salt water at Vũng Tàu, where I gained the faculty to control my body in relation to the sea, which could be overpowering and forgiving in turns. On the way to the shore, my dad would stop to rest at an inactive rubber tree plantation. He would string up a hammock between two sturdy trunks. I recall rubbing my palms

across the trees' bark, my fingertips finding the mucus con-
gealed along deep scores. I pulled at it, peeling it away like skin.
The stench of raw rubber is disgusting. I can smell it even now.
I know now that the revulsion and fascination that the material
aroused in me has a name: the abject. I kneaded the gum and
rolled it into a ball, which bounced delightfully. A whiff of rubber came back to me recently when Lana and I were walking at
Chauncey Peak in Connecticut. The trees in the park were all
aligned in rows that brought back the straight alleys through
which I would chase after my handcrafted rubber ball.

The sand at Vũng Tàu was dirty, unlike the clean white sand
of Pulau Bidong. As refugees, we weren't aware that Malaysia
sheltered not only us but some of the most exquisite tropical
sea life on the planet. What Jim Laurie of ABC News described
as "squalor" and what The New York Times called "Hell Isle" in
1979 is now a coveted spot for deep sea diving. I discovered this
when Lana and I were researching former Vietnamese refugee
camps for our art project.

Once or twice my dad borrowed or rented snorkeling gear
and I rejoiced in floating amid jewellike fish that undulated
like an underwater rainbow—the black domino damsel with
white spots; the tangerine ocellaris clownfish made famous
by Nemo; the parrotfish with lime-green pectoral fins, orange
cheek patches, and red scale margins; and the moon wrasse
with hot pink stripes that mottle its incandescent cyan body and
whose dorsal fin I later found described as having a "magenta

soul, edged with bright blue." Years hence when I studied architecture in college, I won a class competition with my flawless reproduction of all the shades within my classmate's iris. This has led to Lana's entirely unscientific theory that I may owe my color sensitivity to having been immersed in a dazzling spectrum of aquatic pigments at a young age.

Giant sea turtles nested on the other side of the island, which was restricted to prevent anyone from disturbing the protected reptiles. On the forbidden side of the island, offices of the Malaysian officials stood on wooden stilts overlooking the sea. From a distance we could see the humps of sea turtles lazing in the shade under the raised buildings. We understood that the turtles were sacred creatures and should be revered. My research tells me leatherback turtles are the largest turtles on Earth and have roamed the planet for more than 100 million years. They can grow up to seven feet long, weigh over 2,000 pounds, and dive deeper than any other turtle, over 4,000 feet into the ocean depths. There were close to 800 leatherback nestings in Terengganu waters in 1984. But there were more than 4,000 green sea turtles nesting that year, so it is likely that the reptiles I viewed from afar were this equally majestic species. Green turtles are the largest hard-shelled sea turtles and the only herbivores. More petite than the leatherback, they measure three to four feet long and weigh 300 to 350 pounds.

The life history of sea turtles resonates with me, perhaps in the way that Lana identifies with pandas and space aliens. Female marine turtles use an internal compass to locate the electromagnetic signature of their natal beach and must come ashore to nest. The hotter the sand, the faster the embryos develop. Eggs incubated below 82 degrees Fahrenheit will be male and above 88 degrees will be female. In addition to its many other threats, climate change skews the male-to-female ratio of the turtle population, which may hasten the extinction of an already endangered species. Once she has laid her 80 to 120 eggs, the mother never returns to tend the nest. She crawls to the ocean, leaving her hatchlings to the group effort of digging themselves out of the sand cavity and climbing on top of their discarded eggshells to propel themselves out of the chamber. This can take several days. In order to head toward the water, which will save them from dehydration, they move toward the brightest light intensity, which is usually the reflection of the moon on the sea. The chances of a hatchling's survival are one in a thousand.

I never witnessed a hatching, but its drama summons an indelible scene in Tennessee Williams's *Suddenly Last Summer*, which I have never read, but have seen in its movie adaptation on late-night TV. I have been unable to excise from my mind Katherine Hepburn's soliloquy about a sky blackened with flesh-eating birds tearing apart tender sea-turtle hatchlings as they dash across the volcanic beach of the Galapagos Islands. For all the research I have done in the years since departing Pulau Bidong, I have never been able to determine how many Vietnamese attempted to escape: 800,000, a million, two million? Were their chances of survival greater than that of the hatchlings, crammed together, scrambling toward a brighter horizon?

Lulled by the rhythmic pulse of the South China Sea, I breathed in the salty air that tingled in my nostrils. The weather here was clear of the pollution that mired Sài Gòn. When I inhaled, I was buoyed but simultaneously anchored by the oppressive climate that had propelled me to this tranquil yet desolate beach. Here the maelstrom of turmoil, distrust, secrecy, and fear was bizarrely suspended. We, refugees, were in a holding pattern, mourning both pasts and futures lost, grappling to catch our breath, to be able to walk without stumbling. The vastness of the open sea and sky impressed upon me my insignificance. I identified with the crab that burrowed into the sand before being swallowed up by the ocean. But the crabs, like the turtles, were in their natural environment. I couldn't fathom where mine was now that my familiar universe was unreachable. We, humans, have not bred the homing capacities of marine turtles. Perhaps we have cultivated the opposite, making it impossible to return to our natal land. No one had instructed me to, but I shouldered the weight of my forebears. Somehow, I gleaned that I owed a debt to those who did not survive. My family and I had been spared. What then would we do to make good on the promise of freedom?

On Turtle Island beach I collected thin sun-bleached seashells and some of the more intriguing coral shards that washed ashore. I never relinquished my fondness for collecting objects and still cannot resist petrified stones and abandoned nests. I have stashed them in my luggage and carted them from place to place. The nascent sculptor in me recognized these objects as sculpted by nature, but I was also captivated by the ways in which humans repurposed materials. On the island I witnessed an ingenuity sparked by need. Nothing went to waste. This is why I avoided the military man who exploded canisters of food for amusement. Our sardine cans, corn cans, bean cans became different-sized ladles. Cardboard boxes were flattened for bedding. The island taught me an ethics that defied boredom. I was led by a curiosity that had no patience for squandering materials or time. In Sài Gòn I was already accustomed to recycling my old schoolbooks and notebooks, which were sold to make newspapers that might in turn be used for wrapping paper at the market. But it was from the old man at the market who, like a magician, could command a graceful phoenix to rise up out of an empty Coke can using only a pair of rusty scissors that I learned how such transformations attained an artistry beyond mere use.

My family was approved for resettlement in four or five months. The process may have been expedited because my dad had gained favor from officials, but it was more likely because we weren't picky. With four daughters coming of age my dad was not waiting for the prized approval from the U.S. If one of his daughters were to get pregnant, it would change our family's status and delay or jeopardize any resettlement. We left for Montreal in October. I was as sick on the plane as I had been on the boat, maybe even more. Air Canada put us at the very back of a half-empty plane, and though I couldn't keep anything down, filling up bag after bag on the interminable flight, the attendants did not offer a seat closer to the front where I would be less impacted by the turbulence. I hold this against them to this day. Our five tickets were paid through a government loan. It would take six years to repay the government; only then were we able to sponsor our mom and reunite at least part of our family.

When we landed, it was a brisk early fall day, a relief from the muggy triple-digit heat of Kuala Lumpur. The crisp air eased my exhaustion and disorientation. After the onslaught of chaotic, crowded, constricted spaces—from boat to island camp, to transit camp, to airplane—when we arrived at the military barracks in Montreal, the expansive space uplifted me. Amber, vermilion, and auburn leaves, dotted with chartreuse, formed a majestic palette I had yet to behold above water. I was probably as chilled as the time we went for vacation in Đà Lạt up North when I got to buy a new sweater and chose one in cobalt blue, the color of the South China Sea when the sky is clear. We were given long johns, sweaters, and socks, and probably also shoes or boots. We had to handwash our laundry, and as I lay it to dry on the steaming radiators, I observed the differences between men's and women's long johns.

At the camp when fellow refugees heard that we were going to Canada, they warned me, "It's so cold there, your nose and your ears will freeze. When you go back inside, they're going to fall off!" I was horrified at the prospect and anxiously considered how people could live without noses or ears. When I told Lana this story, she was incredulous until she recalled that I also had believed that you could become pregnant if you let a man touch you. When I was riding on a bus headed to ESL school in Vancouver, someone pinched my butt, and I apprehensively awaited my belly growing round. No one had time to explain such things to me. Everyone was preoccupied. On the island, I couldn't query my dad, "Uncle so-and-so says my nose is going to fall off; do we have to go to Canada?" A few weeks after we settled in Vancouver, I discovered my underwear stained with blood. I freaked out and asked my sister Thao what to do. She shoved a sanitary napkin into my hand and told me to put it on. In that sterile modern bathroom, where everything was now blindingly sharp with my new glasses, I felt more in the dark than ever.

•

The first movie I saw in a theater in Canada was *E.T.* Trang had recently settled in Cologne, Germany, and was able to visit us in our basement apartment on Twelfth Avenue. At the theater, all six of us sat in a row. I sobbed in my seat next to Mai, who was probably as overcome as I, although I didn't take notice, so absorbed was I in E.T.'s plight. E.T. was as stranded in the San Fernando Valley as I felt in North America. E.T., the extrater-restrial, resembled a marine reptile, and was as out of place on Earth as a sea turtle on land.

Before my encounter with *E.T.* I had seen only one movie, in a cinema in Sài Gòn. This was the third time I brushed death. My memory is marred by the unruly mass that refused to stand in an orderly line outside the theater. When the doors swung open, the throng poured in, and I was almost crushed under the wave. I wouldn't know that a literal wave would almost over-take me a few years later. As a short eight-year-old, I couldn't see my family above the horde. I was drowning in limbs. Bodies squeezed the breath out of me. Then someone pulled me up.

I can hardly remember the movie because I was so trauma-tized. I recall a fairy tale in which a huntswoman shoots arrows like a female version of Robin Hood and obtains three wishes that come in the form of chestnuts. For forty-five years I have wondered what that movie was. I thought it was likely from the then Soviet Union, or elsewhere in socialist Eastern Europe, which would produce films that the Communist regime would approve to be screened. Lana has figured out that it was a 1973 Czech film by Václav Vorlíček, a co-production with East Germany's DEFA (Deutsche Film-Aktiengesellschaft), whose English title is *Three Wishes for Cinderella* or, sometimes, *Three Nuts for Cinderella*, and the nuts have been variously identified as hazelnuts or acorns. The first nut Cinderella receives contains an entire huntsman's outfit that she dons to impress the prince with her enviable marksmanship. I fixated on this scene and yearned for a bow and arrow for years afterward. I promptly forgot about the other two nuts—one opens up to reveal a ballgown and the other a wedding dress—but I could not forget the handsome chaps that the hunter wore for riding.

I, who would have been a boy in a heartbeat if I could, fulfilling my dad's dreams, never identified with Elliott, the boy who befriends E.T. The nongendered alien was truer to my heart. Though Elliot's sister Gertie asks if E.T. is a boy or a girl, and Elliot replies emphatically that "he" is a boy, I perceived E.T. as gender neutral before the term became popular. That E.T. was neither boy nor girl made all the difference, and though director Steven Spielberg's autobiography bleeds into the script, fashioning it as a boy's coming-of-age story, something about the alien—perhaps that it communicated through seventeen voices, including those of Pat Welsh and Debra Winger, as well as a raccoon, sea otters, and horses—indicates how far E.T. sur-passes human binary gender norms.

When the alien croaked "E.T. phone home," my own throat swelled. The only three words E.T. could speak were like the phrase I croaked when I was rescued from death for the fourth time, "I am door." E.T. spoke my monosyllabic language and was afflicted with the pain of homesickness, a kind of sickness that made missing one's family when you are away at summer camp seem quaint. E.T.'s homesickness had an intergalactic dimension that felt more akin to mine, with my mom oceans away, and my former life impossible to retrieve. E.T.'s make-shift phone, assembled by repurposing a Speak & Spell toy, um-brella, tin foil, and coffee can, reminded me of the ingenious repurposing of humble objects I had seen in Việt Nam and Malaysian refugee camps. The debate over whether Spielberg plagiarized Satyajit Ray's unmade film *The Alien* only confirms how closely the extraterrestrial hewed to my self-identification. Ray described his alien as "a cross between a gnome and a fam-ished refugee child."

Though I never swept past the moon or setting sun, as *E.T.* movie posters depict Eliot and E.T., when I bicycle, I taste a kind of freedom that diverges from the political idea of freedom that is the purported end goal of the refugee's escape. When we landed in Canada, my sisters, dad, and I had attained political freedom. But the taste in my mouth was bile. Political freedom is something you comprehend through legal documents. The freedom that floods my pores when I ride a bike is of a different order. It is not conferred by an external authority but is co-produced between my own energy and my wheeled companion. This species of freedom transported me in Sài Gòn, traveled through me in Vancouver and even the barren suburbs of Mississauga, enabled me to port lumber and supplies during grad school years in California, offered respite from the subway in New York City, and carries me now in Connecticut where I fled for the second time to escape an endangered and constricted life. It is an ephemeral elation that I once fleetingly identified in the figure of an elderly gentleman riding a bicycle.

Not a fan of Steven Spielberg, Lana disdained attending the re-release of *E.T.* for its twentieth anniversary, but she concedes that the film can be unusually affecting for a traumatized former refugee and even a lonely suburban teenager. Lana, too, identified with E.T. because she always felt she came from another planet. Both Lana and I find ourselves more in the alien than in the human characters, though E.T. merges its identity with what must be acknowledged as the creature's love object, producing a plural identity—ElliotT. But the empathic bond between the queer pair must be severed to save the human's life. Before departing the planet and parting from Elliott, E.T. penetrates or impregnates, whichever you prefer, its chosen one with a glowing finger so that Elliott can carry E.T. within him, and indeed we can find ET within ElliotT, just as Lana can be found within Lan Thao. I carry Lana within me and in turn I expand her. Like the collectivity of sea turtles, like Elliott-E.T., Lana and I are at our best as "we."

Yet "we" is such a troubled pronoun; it can exert violence upon those it excludes or presumes to include. On my second trip to New York City, not wanting to make assumptions, I referred to myself and others who were not Lana, as "we."

Through tears, Lana insisted, "I want *us* to be 'we.'"

I did not realize yet that Lana was already inside me. We had found ourselves in and around each other. The first-person-plural pronoun can also invite unbounded pleasures, as Sedgwick extolled, reveling in the permeability of "we." For Sedgwick, "we" is a promiscuous form of world-building. Lana and Lan Thao's mutuality may not be as capacious as what Sedgwick envisioned, but our lives are enriched by the plurality of the other. We have crossed the borders of each other's countries, each carrying our own solitude, yet surviving together for and because of each other.

VII.
AFTER THE WAR

A flash of white will slip past our peripheral vision, or a shadow cross the water. It arrives like a gift. In the morning or at dusk we turn our heads and see a large bird poised upon the pond staring intently below its surface.

On March 9, 2020, I attended a screening of Lana's film *The Cancer Journals Revisited*, a recitation of and rumination upon Audre Lorde's breast cancer memoir and manifesto, which was held at the university where we both teach. We then got on our bikes and rode up the bike path along the Hudson River, stopping to get an espresso at a place I like at Riverside Park and Sixty-eighth Street before completing the rest of the 174-block ride. It was a clear, unseasonably balmy day, atypical of my birthday, which often seems to bring with it bad weather. The next day Lana would host a campus visit for a job search she was chairing. She would go home that Tuesday and periodically attempt to get on the phone with Delta Airlines to change or cancel her flight to Chicago where she had hoped to attend a conference and to see her parents in Naperville, Illinois, something she has never done since I have known her, so it has been over twenty years since she has visited her childhood home.

·

Neither Lana nor I would be back downtown for about a year and a half. The job search Lana was chairing would be canceled. The open studios I had been planning would be delayed for two years. Governor Andrew Cuomo declared a state of emergency on March 7, but Mayor Bill de Blasio would not declare a state of emergency for New York City until March 12, and it would be another eight days before Cuomo announced the lockdown banning "nonessential gatherings of any size for any reason" due to COVID-19.

The university was on spring break the following week, and then the next week became "alternative teaching and learning week" for faculty to prepare for remote instruction until April 12, which then turned into online teaching for the remainder of the semester. This chaotic process came to be known as "pivoting," and Zoom quickly became a household word, at least in the academic realm to which Lana and I belong. I spent twelve hours a day with my eyes adhered to my laptop screen, the days of the week whirring past like microfiche, mechanically propelled by a force that refused to pause and allow any precise moment to come into focus. Lana was coincidentally teaching a seminar on the uncanny; it was as if the world had caught up to her class. She ended up writing a short piece titled "Living in the Uncanny," in which she mourns her abandoned office plants, collateral damage of the pandemic, along with non-COVID related deaths and misery arising from pre-COVID anti-Black racism, overt hostility toward Asians, and mounting anti-Asian violence. The pandemic laid bare the trauma and brutality of the most vulnerable lives, those already suffering systemic harms: Black and brown bodies, disabled bodies, poor bodies, essential workers; none of these categories are exclusive and more often than not they intersect.

Lockdown permitted me to be perpetually embroiled in university affairs while simultaneously brewing shrub so that I could concoct tantalizing cocktails to accompany the meal delivery kits that Lana ordered according to an intricately timed calendar of discounts and free trials. Occasionally the evening "cheer" would leak into our headphones. The first time, we stuck our heads out of the window and climbed onto the fire escape. Lana recorded the clanging pots and pans and somewhat tentative shouts. Up in Washington Heights the ritual never reached the din that we heard on YouTube videos recorded in other neighborhoods. I set up a video camera and recorded the sunset from the window whose view looked out over the rooftops to Wadsworth Avenue where a steady stream of traffic flowed, now uneasily tainted with ambulance lights. The "cheer" went from a curiosity to moving to cruel. How could solidarity descend from a windowsill and be anything more than a performance? Essential workers were either too busy working or too exhausted to care. We lived in a zip code that had among the highest fatality rates in the city, because there were so many immigrants there who were essential workers.

To the unremitting scream of sirens, Lana panic-bought two liters of hand sanitizer. One of them remains unopened more than two years since its purchase and currently props up a Taiwanese hand puppet of the King of the Gods. She also bought several cans of corn and tomatoes that have likewise gone unopened, save for one can of corn that I deemed tasteless. Trips to take out the garbage and do laundry became treacherous for fear of the inevitable encounter with someone unmasked. Jogging in the overcrowded park became untenable and walks joyless. Being locked down also meant feeling locked in. When the subway shut down overnight for the first time in its history, it marked the end of something. For Lana, at least, the city of her youth, where she forged something she began to recognize as her "self," was extinguished, possibly irrevocably.

By mid-April, NYC had surpassed 10,000 deaths from COVID-19, and by the end of the month *The New York Times* was running grisly headlines of funeral homes in Brooklyn with "bodies . . . coming out of our ears." The escalation of deaths was so sudden that the goal of "flattening" the curve seemed unreachable. In retrospect the "crisis" period was compressed into two months. By mid-June, NYC had its first day since the start of the pandemic with only one reported COVID death. But a vaccine was as yet unimaginable. No one could predict the mercurial behavior of a virus that still seemed as unfathomable as an invasion from outer space. Most New Yorkers were in a state of shock. Most New Yorkers, Lana lamented, had already fled, at least the New Yorkers we knew. It then became uncomfortably clear that who we knew had the means to flee, either through financial capital or proximity to financial capital in some form or another.

Though it wasn't entirely true, Lana felt that her closest friends had all escaped New York. Lana's sister Cynthia and her husband owned a building in Bushwick and had kept the rooftop apartment for themselves, so they at least had some private contact with the open air. But the crux of Lana's resentment hardened around her eldest sister JuPong who, from Lana's perspective, enjoyed a palatial house in Amherst, Massachusetts, and for her parents, who enabled JuPong to live beyond the means of a faculty member at a low-residency art program, beyond what Lana and I could afford on our two full-time salaries.

I placed Lana's bike on a trainer, and she would pedal while frantically scrolling through my Zillow account, seeking a refuge. Lana had been teaching for over twenty years, during which time she had gone up for tenure twice at two different institutions and had never been granted an academic leave. I had applied for teaching jobs for fourteen years before securing my present full-time teaching appointment. We had miraculously managed to synchronize our first-ever academic leaves for the upcoming year in order to complete a commission for KW Gallery in Berlin. Now Lana was on a mission, initially to find a tenable working space within walking distance, but when this more modest goal was unattainable, her desperation fueled an urgency to find a place where we could not only labor but also repose, where we could not only survive but savor our lives and breathe freely. We were in our early and mid-fifties. Among the deaths that year were three friends and acquaintances who were significantly younger than Lana. Their passing weighed upon her. She heard the refrain of a passage in her film, spoken by a forensic psychologist who suffered from life-altering cancer twice: "What we have is now." This line pierces me as well. There may not be a long road ahead, Lana surmised.

In one of the red-and-black notebooks that she bought in Chinatown during her early days in New York, Lana conjectured that she was small enough to fit inside another person. She had been encouraged not to trouble the world, to slip through life as complacently as possible, not to disturb the universe with demands for change, desires for sustenance. The Asians now protesting in the streets clamoring for respect, recognition, and dignity in solidarity with Black folx inspired her. When would she be able to count herself among the deserving, to consider her life as "real" as others' lives, even as "living history," as Alice B. Toklas remarked on the process of typing Gertrude Stein's *The Making of Americans*? I didn't want Lana to be small enough to fit inside me. I wanted her to bear her own weight, and for us to carry ourselves together.

Lana drew a circle around NYC with a two-hour public transportation commute radius. She input our maximum budget and multiple other parameters in her self-made algorithm. She reloaded Zillow continually and every night she would show me results, and I would shake my head "no." If Lana had one criterion—no mildew—mine was that when I approached the house I wanted to feel happy to be home; I wanted the house to enrapture me. No real estate broker, family member, or even friend could intuit this subjective bar. Even Lana was at times outraged at its nebulousness, but she was determined. As midnight neared on her birthday eve, trying to subdue her excitement, she waited for me to log off Zoom and stagger out of my bedroom office. Although it was late and I was spent, she compelled me to look at the listing for her birthday. She offered me her chair so I could click through the images of a former sawmill in Connecticut from the 1700s. I was stunned at the waterfall, the pond, the stone walls, the cedar shingles. It was a modest house that I would be gratified to come home to. "This will not last," I pronounced.

We spent Lana's birthday obtaining a pre-approval letter to view the property, a requirement meant to prohibit idle curiosity in the historic house. Two days later we took the Metro-North to New Haven, rented a car, and drove up, running late, to park in a long driveway already filling up with cars. A broker who was attached to the property on Zillow hurried us in, but not before Lana caught sight of a stone rabbit guarding the front door. "Does this come with the house?" Lana pleaded, her heart pounding at the prospect. It was close to 90 degrees, and the blazing sun glinted in the water that bubbled over the moss-covered stone wall fountain feature. The broker's mask, imprinted with her company's logo, kept falling below her nose as she escorted us through the Dutch door and across a wooden bridge where we paused to stare at the minnow swimming below. It felt like we had walked into a fairy tale, except that we kept bumping into other prospective buyers. Inside, wide plank floors were held down with antique square-cut nails, the wood showing evidence of wood-boring insects of unknown origin. There was a landing with a wooden rail where we could look down to the floor below, reminding me of the house in Sài Gòn where my dad had designed the retractable skylight to vent smoke from the kitchen stove.

We climbed down the steep stairs, neither of us touching the rope that served as a handrail, and caught up with the broker who was pointing at the stone wall in the finished basement that the owners had been calling "the great room." She told us that the mill was designed so that Jepp Brook would run beneath the structure. Later the inspector would lift the hatch in the floor, and I would put on a headlight, so, like a miner, I could descend into the depths, cooled by the damp air before I could register the water flow. When we subsequently uncovered the portal to show friends, I noticed a light-colored stone. Lana and I fell silent at its resemblance to a marble Buddha head that we had set on the fireplace mantle. The mill had in place its guardians both above and below.

Water was everywhere—around, inside, and underneath the house. This was bound to cause problems. In retrospect, we understood why the broker had initiated our phone inquiry with a warning: "You will need flood insurance." The mustiness was strong enough to penetrate at least Lana's mask, and the stone wall over which the pond water cascaded was of uncertain stability. Misgivings multiplied and we returned to NYC dejected. That evening we played the video that Lana had recorded, and it brought tears to my eyes. I could envision the great room as a real artist's studio, the garage could double as a shop, and Lana could use the living room as an office. Our impetus for attending the open house was the chance to breathe, and what we found was breathtaking.

The following morning the broker texted to let us know that an offer had been made and to ask if we wanted to put in one as well. We decided we would go no higher than the asking price. Even this would put a huge strain on our budget, but we expected that it would be insufficient. Sending our offer, as if guided by an external agency, I typed: "We would be honored to be the new stewards of the mill." Because I never consulted Lana about this final promise, I bear this mantle on my own.

On the landing between what is now our bedroom and the bathroom stands a wall whose paint is duller than its neighbor's but that cannot be refreshed or torn down to enlarge the bathroom. In the manner by which a child's growth is marked, the wall archives the occupants of the mill dating back to 1958, as far as I have deciphered. One month after we closed on the house, I held a ruler atop Lana's head and drew a line for her to imprint her name. She did the same for me, and I inscribed my name next to hers, but slightly higher. We debated about whether the ruler had been held evenly or the floor sloped. We were now agents in the "living history" of the mill.

Light travels the ceiling at the mill, measuring time. Sine waves wave signs to me. The old glass in the twenty-four windows with their deteriorating frames produces mesmerizing reflections that ripple across the walls. Every time we tire of the trials here—the war with snakes, raccoons, mice, geese, carpenter ants, powderpost beetles, and spiders whose webs would overtake us if I didn't periodically destroy their homes—the mill turns around and says, *Here is how I uplift you; I can revitalize you.* I find myself peering at the sky in a way I haven't before, as a space of respite, of possibility. A red-shouldered hawk lands on the sloped wooden bridge; painted turtles swiftly slip off their logs into the murky protection of the pond. The waterfall rages, a dull white noise, rumbling, always present until the driest summer months when it dwindles to a trickle. Fireflies occasionally dot the landscape. I mistake them momentarily for car lights. On July 4 we stand on the bridge, watching bursts of light peek through tree branches. Green frogs bleat, and after the sun sets and the heat wanes, katydids sing in unison. Once in dark of night the motion sensor light at the garage suddenly illuminated, casting a spotlight upon the silhouette of a deer and its mate gracefully treading across the snow.

At the mill Lana wakes and ponders aloud, "What's playing at the pond?" First, she goes to the kitchen to put on the kettle for tea and coffee, and then she barges into the living room, now her office, to throw open the Dutch door that looks onto the pond. After observing a winged creature as it flies over the treetops, she takes to tiptoeing into the pond-side room, not wanting to startle any potential visitors.

The great blue heron looks like a primitive species, kin of the pterodactyl, as if it comes from another planet, another time. This is perhaps why Lana and I are both transfixed by it. Lana created a file of heron sightings: *7/30/2020 once; 8/4/20 once; 8/12/20 morning and dusk; 8/14/20 @ 11:12 A.M. and 11:17 A.M.; 8/20/20; 8/26 10:07 A.M. flying overhead; 9/2/20; 9/3/20; 9/6/20; 9/8/20 5:47 P.M.; 9/13/20 9:38 A.M.; 9/20/20 around 5/5:30 P.M.; 9/24?/20 flock of 5–7 cranes or egrets fly overhead, and then a heron; 9/30/20 around 3 P.M. a large heron dives down toward the water and flies low toward our lawn side of the pond and away. We are on the porch, LT giving me my first outdoor haircut at the Mill; 10/4/20 at dusk; 11/4/20 3:58 P.M. Maybe it's a good sign, on this strange day after the election, awaiting the fate of the world, it seems; 11/19/20 11:11 A.M; 3/18/21 close to dusk; 4/2/21 heron swoops down and lands on a branch; 4/7/21 Heron at around 5 P.M at the pond. It slowly makes its way around the pond, walking, poking its beak out. It looks 2-dimensional when it comes toward you and then turns 3D. Prehistoric looking, supernatural, and mythic; 9:30 A.M 7/8/21 big thunderstorm because of tropical storm Elsa, great blue heron stopped by in the pouring rain.*

Nothing natural casts a shadow on the pond as large as a heron. A heron can reach a height as tall as Lana and me, and its average wingspan would be taller. Its white chest is dappled with gray flecks and swatches of pink tuck into its wings. Rosewood feathers on the top of its legs give the impression of pantaloons. Yesterday I saw one plunge into the water three times, coming up empty. Its feathers sopping, it ruffled them like a parasol, drying itself out. It shook out its wings with the motion of drying one's back with a towel. The heron combines the extremes of comic and regal like nothing else I've seen. It uses its foot to scratch behind its ear, which I assume it has, though I have yet to find definitive confirmation, and then pokes at its chest with its bill. It elongates its neck and strikes a pose. Minutes later it scrunches itself into a quarter of its size, reminding me of a grumpy old man.

What goes through the mind of a wading bird as it stands with its head held aloft, bill level to the surface of the water, as if listening to the wind? My sensory knowledge of *Ardea herodias* is limited to sight, and occasionally to hearing. I have heard them cawing—or should I say cackling?—in their rookery atop the trees that bank Lake Whitney. *The Old Farmer's Almanac* reports that as they land in the nest they call to their partner with a "squawking roh-roh-roh." But at our pond they are silent. I hear only the splash when one plunges for prey, never as it paces the pool's marshy edges, dragging aquatic sinews behind its algae-coated feet.

Joyce Carol Oates wrote a short story titled "Great Blue Heron" in which a woman notes that the great blue heron is not blue. The woman, a recent widow, finds it "eerie and unsettling"—Lana might say "uncanny"—that the creature does not use its wings to fly but walks "like a human being in some way handicapped or disfigured." (This is because what appear to be knees that bend backward are more like human ankle joints.) The mourning woman begins to take on the characteristics of a heron, or wish for them. To be a predator. In a dream she becomes a giant great blue heron raining terror upon six boys who throw rocks at her lake's waterfowl.

The heron can hunt by moonlight with UV-sensitive vision, but more often it stalks its prey at dawn and twilight. The kill always happens with lightning speed, a precision that belies the bird's comedic failures. A slosh alerts you if you have let your attention flag. The predatory avian, whose head sometimes resembles a bullet with a dagger-sharp beak, lunges forward as if its neck were spring loaded, and its catch is thrust into its supple throat. The obstruction in its gullet protrudes and wriggles as the heron reflexively forces it into its flexible cavity. When it opens its mouth to reveal the bright yellow interior, it looks as if it were laughing. The bird cleans itself, forming its neck into a figure eight. A single feather is plucked loose and floats out on the reservoir, placing its signature upon the pond as ours are on the wall of names at the landing. Reflections from the water dance on its tufted chest as it awaits its next prey.

We reached a pinnacle of heron obsession when we tracked down a heronry or rookery at Lake Whitney where there were perhaps as many as twenty herons in at least six nests atop a cluster of trees on one side of the lake, and at least three nests on the other side. Purring, whining, screeching, and honking cascaded from the upper branches.

The heron will always outdo us in patience. We become absorbed in other things, urgent or trifling. I reenter the room and catch only the dilating ripples on the water that signal a departure. There is no forewarning. Like Lana, I always feel a bit deflated when I miss its leaving, which I almost always do. Lana bemoans, "I didn't have a chance to say goodbye."

Like the widow in Oates's story, like my mom alone in Mississauaga, like the many people single or separated during the lockdown, the heron is a solitary creature. There is never more than one on the pond at a time.

Lana has been told that she carries her solitude with her, even as she and I have sustained a relationship of twenty-two years. She is not a solitary creature, but she did grow up in solitude. Her sense of abandonment appears to arrive with the flight of an avian who does not bid her farewell, but its origins can be tracked to parents who, though faultless providers, left their young to scavenge on their own.

He has left. He has gone. He will not be returning. These are words the widow in Oates's story repeats to herself, a refrain that tolled in my head as I submitted to COVID-19 testing to cross the U.S.-Canadian border for my father's funeral, and that still echoes in my head when I put on his T-shirt and boxer shorts, which fit me well, as he had grown so frail, and I have gotten a little heftier.

From Lana I have gleaned that the uncanny is the familiar made strange. In his essay "The 'Uncanny,'" Freud traces the etymology of *heimlich* (homely) to its purported opposite, *unheimlich* (unhomely or uncanny), which it unexpectedly contains, revealing how intimacy and fraternity coexist with difference and antagonism. The uncanny lurks behind why we feel unsettled by the foreign and why confronting the other fills us with dread. Jordan Peele's 2019 film *Us* provided a creepy climax to the seminar Lana was teaching when New York City went into lockdown. A parable of American capitalist terror where underground enslaved doppelgangers rebel against their surface counterparts, Peele's dystopian science fiction adeptly maintains ambiguity as to who is "us" and who is "them." Far too disturbing for Lana to consciously identify with, the film nevertheless seeped under her skin. She had never felt that she was "us." She was always one of "them." To witness the world veer into the uncanny at the upsurge of the pandemic shifted its power balance for her. She had identified herself as uncanny to others, but now that everyday life had become uncanny, she glimpsed an opening, an invitation not just to embrace difference but perhaps even incite antagonism.

On January 15, 2022, Michelle Alyssa Go was fatally pushed onto the train tracks at Times Square. When I heard of the horrific incident, I redoubled my warnings to Lana, whose mind is usually elsewhere when she paces on a subway platform, buried in a book or her phone, burrowed into her own world. Though police reports at the time indicated that the violence did not originate in anti-Asian hate, photographs circulated online memorializing the forty-year-old woman as another victim of escalating anti-Asian violence. Horror-stricken, Lana noticed that Go was wearing a striped boat neck shirt from Uniqlo that she also owns. On the second anniversary of her death, scans of the photo, protected in a plastic sleeve, were taped to I-beams on the uptown R train platform at Union Square station. The image of Go in this shirt is now on the Death of Michelle Go Wikipedia page. The page lists the motive for her murder as "Possibly anti-Asian racism."

There's something distinctly unsettling about seeing a person who died a brutal death at the hands of an unprovoked attacker clothed in attire that hangs in your own closet. Go's hair is long and straight, parted slightly off-center to the left. This is how Lana wore hers when she was in junior high, although parted slightly off-center to the right. Lana would probably say that Go looks like a younger, happier version of herself, if she had kept her hair long. Those who knew Go reported that she was jolly, a word never used to describe Lana. A neighbor said, "She was just the person who did everything right." This, Lana could imagine, others might say of her. If not doing everything right, at least trying to. It was what she was told to do by her parents, if not in words, then by every other means of communication. Doing everything right was how she was brought up. But the pandemic broke that impulsive drive. The Asian blaming, the Asian beating, the Asian deaths crushed Lana's need to do the right thing, blotted out her belief that doing the right thing would somehow earn her the right to be rewarded. It couldn't even earn you the right to live and breathe.

One month later, Christina Yuna Lee would be stabbed more than forty times in her Chinatown apartment building. And two months later, eight people would be slaughtered, six of them Asian women, in what has come to be known as the Atlanta Spa Shootings.

The mill offered a haven from Lana's deep-rooted anger with her biological family, but a month into our seclusion, Lana was put in touch with them when she was contacted by a potential buyer of property in Florida that her parents had bought in their progeny's names. The land was of very little value and the amount of tax that her parents had paid for property that they never resided on nor developed far exceeded its worth. All three Lin daughters were willing to sell their plots, but the offer was withdrawn when active gopher tortoise burrows were found on site.

Lana was deeply moved that the land she had presumed to be a waste had actually been generative over the years. She identified with this unassuming and vulnerable yet enduring creature. Its burrows of up to forty feet sustain more than 300 species that make their homes in longleaf pine savannahs. The gopher tortoise has therefore attained the status of a Florida keystone species. The threatened and protected reptile can only thrive in forests with an open understory because it cannot forage for food where there is too much overgrowth, and tortoise eggs are incubated by the sun, which must be able to reach the burrow openings.

Lana pauses at the mention of "understory." Her ears catch the hint of narrative from whose web she has tried throughout her life to extricate herself, but which repeatedly draws her back. Much as she continually rejects the category of "storyteller" to describe herself, I believe it is her karmic debt to struggle with the scripting of stories. Both the first job search she chaired and the most recent have been for some form of storyteller, and I predict they will not be her last.

"Metaphorically," Robert MacFarlane writes in *Underland: A Deep Time Journey*, "the 'understory' is . . . the sum of the entangled, ever-growing narratives, histories, ideas, and words that interweave to give a wood or forest its diverse life in culture." MacFarlane ventures into the woods with a plant wizard named Merlin and together they observe a beech tree whose branches have fused. They debate whether this process is called pleaching or snogging or inosculation, from the Latin *osculare*, meaning "to kiss." Regardless of the precise term, the kissing boughs present an occasion to reflect upon the qualities of living wood, which, like water, will eventually flow, if at a glacial pace. MacFarlane goes on to invoke Ursula K. Le Guin's *The Word for World Is Forest*, an anti-colonial, anti-logging, anti-military science fiction critique. Translating Le Guin's word for "world" into Chinese it becomes Lin or Lam, both of which mean "wood" or "forest." Lam is the Cantonese version of Lin. Together Lana and I make our world, and like the forest and its understory, we are interwoven, interdependent, speaking to one another in a language only we can understand.

A beech tree, at least seventy years old, stretches out its limbs on our small plot of yard. Ten feet in girth, it soars beyond our means of measuring—fifty feet or more? Beneath its canopy of branches that has shielded me in mild rain, I set up an open-air office, no longer Zooming next to my bed. No pleaching or inosculation have we witnessed; instead, it is Lana and I who kiss, who grow separately but not apart.

A friend tells us that "beech" is the Proto-Germanic word for "book." How fitting that this arboreal creature opens its arms to us as a book. We are new to its language and cannot read its story, but it would not be surprising if it could read ours, sensing in its wordless wisdom a yearning to interleave our histories. Also fitting, the beech is hermaphroditic, its flowers neither male nor female but monoecious. It spews its tassel-like catkins across the yard and pond, cloaking them with a slightly fuzzy blanket. And then in the fall, we, mostly I, rake beechnuts into heaps, collect them into a wheelbarrow, cart them to the town side of our lot, and release them to potentially propagate. Lana and I have no offspring. On what I was afraid to admit was our first date, we discussed our mutual disinterest in breeding. Our duty may instead be to sustain the wildlife around us and to labor for its procreation.

This past spring, however, our majestic guardian was attacked by nematodes. Or is it only now that we have read its distress signals in shriveled and striped leaves? In three years, Lana and I have seen this specimen tree tower ever closer to the clouds. The prospect of losing it pains us. How to protect our mill's protector from this invasion? Our arborist has nursed the copper beech since it was a sapling, watering it with a can filled at the pond. He used to enjoy the view of the waterfall from the top bunk in his grandmother's guestroom, a room we have now labeled "studio B." He cannot guarantee the success of the experimental treatments for beech leaf disease but promises to do what he can for his childhood companion.

Recently Lana heard that LGBTQ Vietnamese have devised a pronoun for nonbinary persons–*chanh*, which is a combination of *chị* (sister) and *anh* (brother). It is an interesting choice because chanh is the word for "lemon," which is itself a hybrid species. Although I had not heard of the term—I don't keep up with Vietnamese colloquialisms—I have affection for it because it takes the name of a fruit, my favorite food group. In English slang, "fruit" can be used to refer to gay men. Fruit also acquires a ghastly meaning in Billie Holiday's recording of Lewis Allan's (Abel Meeropol's) poem then song, "Strange Fruit." The bitter association between Black lynching and fruit cannot be expunged. There is poignancy to the capacity of this humble word to carry the fraught histories of outcasts.

It occurs to me that the names of fruit often reflect their color: lemon, orange, grape, lime, even strawberry. According to Maggie Nelson, who writes about the pain of blue in *Bluets*, one of Gertrude Stein's primary concerns in *Tender Buttons* is hurt colors. Nelson goes on to scan her room of students, like Lana, possibly for affirmation, when she quotes Stein: "Enthusiastically hurting a clouded yellow bud and saucer."

Since our trip to Việt Nam, I have contemplated a project on the color yellow. I ported an expensive tub of gamboge, a saffron pigment, back to New York with me, and it is now sitting in the garage at the mill. Taking its name from *Camboja*, an old form of Cambodia or Kampuchea, as the country is known by its people, gamboge is harvested in a manner similar to rubber. The paint pigment derives from the sap of the tree of the genus *Garcinia*, a species of which produces the mangosteen fruit that I adore, although *Garcinia mangostana* exudes an inferior quality gamboge. My dormant project means to investigate the intertwined histories of painting, war, and colonialism through the color yellow.

When Europeans came to identify skin with color tones and claimed the color white, deeming the other skin tones black, yellow, and red, they produced a colorized racial hierarchy. The racist metaphor of a "yellow peril" emerged out of this history of colonialism. To produce the pigments that would render skin tones, British companies such as Winsor & Newton financed the harvesting of resin from trees in Southeast Asia. Ian Garrett, former technical director of Winsor & Newton, declared on the podcast *Radiolab*, "People who paint don't tend to start wars." While this may be true, people who paint can benefit from war, or, to think of this another way, paint can be a byproduct of people who make war. Paint can be as tainted as blood money. Gamboge was very rare during the wars in Việt Nam and Cambodia because of the landmines that prevented its collection. Supplies of "dirty gamboge" were found to contain exploded bullets. The brilliant yellow highlights in J. M. W. Turner's famous *Slave Ship* painting may draw their dangerous power from this legacy of colonial violence. If colors can hurt, gamboge certainly knows this sorrow.

Reflecting upon the potency and politics of color, it does not escape my attention that my green card, finally secured in 2021, gains its name from a color. My quest for a green card was indeed painful. As Kermit the Frog complains, "It's not easy bein' green." The pale green Form 1–151 Alien Registration Receipt Card emerged in 1940 when foreign-born persons over fourteen years old were required to report to a U.S. Post Office and register their presence to the government of the United States. The card was redesigned seventeen times between 1952 and 1977 to combat counterfeiting. My green card is, in fact, green, but between 1977 and May 2010 the green card wasn't even green.

Despite the unease of the hue of envy, "people's desire for green," as Victoria Finlay puts it in her natural history of the palette, may prevail unquenched since antiquity. Such covetousness most often takes the material form of money in contemporary times, but in ancient China there was a mysterious, sought-after color found on porcelain. The celadon glaze on Song Dynasty pottery, carrying decorative flaws like veins that emulate snowflakes, tortoise shells, or river networks, is alive, like wood, and continues to crack for some time after firing.

From a Buddhist monk Finlay hears a story about celadon green that resonates with me. A deity arrives in a boy's dream and tells him how to attain everything he's ever wanted. The child is instructed to close his eyes and not think about green. The boy shuts his eyes and all he can think of is the sea and the tide. As he grows older, he tries again from time to time but can never prevent his mind from returning to green. When he becomes an aged man, he closes his eyes one last time and then opens them smiling, for he realizes he now has everything he always wanted. I am like both the boy and the man, whom I have always wished to be. I see the green of the South China Sea and of the algae-covered pond and hemlock and spruce trees around me, but when I see green, I understand that I have everything I have always wanted. For over two decades I sought the security of green; now green crackles around Lana and me, imperfect, flawed, and ever fulfilling.

In her autobiography *What Is Remembered*, Alice B. Toklas writes of Chinese servants who are peripheral to the central protagonists in her story, similar to the "Indo-Chinese" servants in Stein's *Everybody's Autobiography*. After the 1906 San Francisco earthquake, Alice's friend Nellie's Chinese cook housed thirty of his cousins in Nellie's basement. The earthquake did not cause serious structural damage, but it broke the water mains, and explosions set with the intention of squelching the fire instead caused new fires that burned for four days and nights, destroying Chinatown. The catastrophe accomplished the relocation of Chinese that some had already advocated, as indicated in a 1905 *Merchants Association Review* headline that refers to Chinatown as a "standing menace" from which San Francisco might be freed. Alice says nothing about this aspect of the disaster except for a parenthetical quip about subterranean "refugees" who hid so quietly that no one discovered them until weeks had passed. My affinity for the undetected

Chinese refugees sequestered in the basement is an impetus for this book, for bringing the understory to the surface.

Jeanette Winterson's *Oranges Are Not the Only Fruit* is the first English-language book that had a profound impact on me, that showed me what could be done with language, that it needn't only be literal but could strive for metaphorical depth; it introduced me to queer desire and gave me words for that as well. Lana and I visited Winterson's shop in Spitalfields that season we spent in London during Lana's post-cancer PhD research-and-writing phase. It had little meaning for Lana, since at that time she had never read any Winterson. But reading had always been an escape for Lana, especially when she was a child. As Winterson puts it, reading opens the hidden door of a book for the story to understand us, to see us, to make us feel seen. Close to three decades after *Oranges* was published, the author reflected upon the oft-asked question of why she insists that her book is a novel and not a memoir. Winterson explains that she sought to expand the "I" such that "I am I and I am Not-I." This claim arises from the fact that life is "part fact part fiction."

I am I and I am Not-I. To my ears, this echoes psychoanalyst/pediatrician D. W. Winnicott's formulation of the transitional object that is both the "me" of the baby and "not me," something in between the child and the autonomous teddy bear or stuffed monkey. I am I, Lan Thao Lam, and I am Not-I,

Lana Lin. Perhaps in some ways we are transitional objects for one another, allowing ourselves to live in transition, to and from ourselves and each other, in the between.

•

It may have been on that first long walk we took in Toronto, or not long after, that Lana floated the idea of *The Autobiography of H. Lan Thao Lam*. She enjoyed the rhythm of the title. It surprised me until she explained how the project would mimic Gertrude Stein's composition of *The Autobiography of Alice B. Toklas*. For the next twenty years it came up now and then, until Lana announced that it was time that the book was written or both of us would be too enfeebled to recall who we were and what we had been through. It may be that a great love is shown through listening to another's story. It may be that a greater love still is shown through telling another's story. A different kind of love arises when merging another's story with one's own.

Throughout the process of this book's composition Lana has protested that she was writing herself out of existence. Now she ponders whether she has written herself into existence. It is a mystery. The puzzle reminds her of a strange window display that we happened upon one evening when we strolled past a store that sold notions and knitting paraphernalia. A knitted monkey seated in a flying saucer was knitting itself into being.

The display was especially uncanny to us, for I am a monkey in Chinese astrology, and Lana is branded with a flying saucer birthmark on her back. In our personal mythology we fantasize that when it is time for her alien brood to depart this planet, I will accompany Lana. There will be no basement, no "below-deck" in our space vessel. I will be seated beside her as copilot.

About three years ago, Lana Lin said, "I am going to write *The Autobiography of H. Lan Thao Lam* as simply as Stein did *The Autobiography of Alice B. Toklas*." And she has and this is it.

WORKS CITED

Biss, Eula. *Notes From No Man's Land: American Essays*. Minneapolis: Graywolf Press, 2009.

Dickinson, Emily. 1861. "I'm Nobody! Who are you?" Themorgan. org. Accessed October 6, 2024. https://www.themorgan.org/exhibitions/online/emily-dickinson/11.

Didion, Joan. "Goodbye to All That." In *Slouching Towards Bethlehem*. New York: Farrar, Straus and Giroux, 1968.

Finlay, Victoria. *Color: A Natural History of the Palette*. New York: Random House, 2003.

Fishkin, Shelley Fisher and Maxine Hong Kingston. "Interview with Maxine Hong Kingston." *American Literary History* 3, no. 4 (1991): 782–91.

Freud, Sigmund. 1919. "The 'Uncanny.'" In *An Infantile Neurosis and Other Works (1917–1919): The Standard Edition of the Complete Psychological Works of Sigmund Freud* (Volume 17), edited by James Strachey. London: Hogarth Press, 1955.

Lorde, Audre. *The Cancer Journals*. San Francisco: Spinster's Ink, 1980.

Majmudar, Amit. "Five Famous Asian War Photographs." In *The Best American Essays*, edited by Hilton Als and Robert Atwan. Boston: Mariner Books, 2018.

Marker, Chris, dir. *La Jetée*. Argos Films, 1962.

Macfarlane, Robert. *Underland: A Deep Time Journey*. New York: W. W. Norton, 2019.

Min, Katherine. 2005. "Of Anger and Ambivalence." Katherinekmin.com. Accessed October 6, 2024. https://katherinekmin.com/of-anger-and-ambivalence/.

Mosel, Arlene. *Tikki Tikki Tembo*. New York: Holt, Rinehart and Winston, 1968.

Nelson, Maggie. *Bluets*. Seattle: Wave Books, 2009.

Oates, Joyce Carol. "Great Blue Heron." In *Dis Mem Ber: And Other Stories of Mystery and Suspense*. New York: Mysterious Press, 2017.

Sedgwick, Eve Kosofsky. *Tendencies*. Durham, North Carolina: Duke University Press, 1993.

Socarides, Alexandra. "The Poems (We Think) We Know: Emily Dickinson." *Los Angeles Review of Books,* June 25, 2014. Accessed October 6, 2024. https://lareviewofbooks.org/article/poems-think-know-emily-dickinson/.

Sontag, Susan. *On Photography*. New York: Delta, 1977.

Stein, Gertrude. (1933) *The Autobiography of Alice B. Toklas*. New York: Vintage Books/Random House, 1961.

___. *Everybody's Autobiography*. New York: Vintage, 1973.

Tan, Amy. (1989) *The Joy Luck Club*. New York: Random House, 2008.

___. *Where the Past Begins: Memory and Imagination*. New York: HarperCollins, 2017.

Toklas, Alice B. *The Alice B. Toklas Cook Book*. New York: HarperCollins, 1984.

___. *What Is Remembered*. New York: Holt, 1963.

Truong, Monique. *The Book of Salt*. New York: Houghton Mifflin Harcourt, 2004.

Winterson, Jeanette. "Introduction." In *Oranges Are Not the Only Fruit*. University of Chicago Press, 2014.

Yoshino, Kenji. *Covering: The Hidden Assault on Our Civil Rights*. New York: Random House, 2011.

ACKNOWLEDGEMENTS

This book emerged from its private gestation through the wisdom, guidance, and camaraderie of my evolving women of color writing group: Jackie Wang, Rose Rejouis, Mahreen Sohail, Chet'la Sebree; and Lily Hoang, whose careful reading and scrupulous feedback was crucial to its development.

Thank you to Porochista Khakpour for insights and encouragement at a time of need.

My immense gratitude to Danielle Dutton and Martin Riker for believing in this project and understanding it, at times better than I felt I did myself, and for the best editorial experience of my life. I couldn't ask for a better home for this work.

I am indebted to Shannon Mattern for championing my work on so many occasions, Melissa Friedling for comradeship at our day jobs that enabled me to preserve the inner resources needed to complete this project, Julia Foulkes for support at the proposal stage, Margaret Rhee for ceaseless enthusiasm, and Kate Eichhorn for caffeinated consultation. Thank you to my research assistants, B.A. Williams and Lananh Chu. Lala, I am so grateful for your meticulous attention on this project and others.

A sabbatical from The New School, albeit at the height of the 2020 COVID pandemic, allowed me to make significant strides in this work, and residency in the charming stone Veltin studio at Mac-Dowell gave me the time and fortitude to realize the first full draft.

To my biological, extended, and chosen families: I humbly thank you for all you have done for me.

To my person, my home, my fellow passenger: thank you for the privilege of sharing your life/our lives, of borrowing your name, of telling and embellishing y/our story. This book, and life itself in its most treasured meanings, would quite literally not be possible without you. I will await you or expect you to wait for me in the spaceship.

ABOUT THE AUTHOR

Lana Lin is a writer, artist, and filmmaker based in New York and Connecticut. She is the author of the book *Freud's Jaw and Other Lost Objects: Fractured Subjectivity in the Face of Cancer* and film and video works including *The Cancer Journals Revisited.* Her various works and collaborative projects (with Lan Thao Lam as "Lin + Lam") have been exhibited at festivals and art and educational spaces throughout the world, including the Museum of Modern Art, Whitney Museum, and New Museum, New York; the National Gallery of Art, Washington, D.C.; Gasworks, London; the Taiwan International Documentary Festival and Taiwan Film and Audiovisual Institute, New Taipei City; Arko Art Center, Korean Arts Council, Seoul; and the 2018 Busan Biennale. Having had three years of psychoanalytic training before dropping out, she sometimes still dreams of becoming a psychoanalyst one day.

DOROTHY, A PUBLISHING PROJECT